Perils of
Professionalism

Perils of Professionalism

Essays on Christian Faith and Professionalism

Donald B. Kraybill and Phyllis Pellman Good, Editors

HERALD PRESS
Scottdale, Pennsylvania
Kitchener, Ontario
1982

Library of Congress Cataloging in Publication Data
Main entry under title:

Perils of professionalism.

1. Professions—Social aspects—Addresses, essays,
lectures. 2. Professions—Religious aspects—Christ-
ianity—Addresses, essays, lectures. 3. Professions—
Religious aspects—Mennonites—Addresses, essays,
lectures. I. Kraybill, Donald B. II. Good, Phyllis
Pellman.
HT687.P47   261.8'34553   82-3052
ISBN 0-8361-1997-5 (pbk.)   AACR2

Chapter 18 is reprinted with minor changes by
permission of the author and the publisher from
*Nonresistance and Responsibility and Other Mennonite
Essays* by Gordon Kaufman, copyright 1979 by Faith and
Life Press, Newton, Kansas.

82   83   84   85   86   87   88   10   9   8   7   6   5   4   3   2   1

Contents

Introduction

Professionalism abounds all around us. A higher proportion of the labor force today is labeled professional than ever before. Many occupational groups want to be called professional. Virtually everyone is concerned about projecting a "professional image" and acting in a professional manner. The term "unprofessional" competes in our society with the word sin as the prime symbol of evil and the demonic. Yet surprisingly little has been written or said about the relationship between Christian faith and professionalism. We hope that this book can be a small step in that direction.

Scholarly students of the professions may be disappointed with our collection since we do not plow any new academic furrows. We have moved in a different direction by assembling articles and stories written by practicing professionals for other practicing professionals and laypersons. The writers contributing to this collection are not "experts" in the scientific study of professions. They are professional experts in other fields who, for the most part, have written about their own experience. We have asked them *not* to write about specific problems within their own profession. We have rather encouraged them to address a general question about professionalism which is also relevant to many other professions, while drawing freely on their own working knowledge of a particular profession for illustrations. Our contributors have dealt with the specific, the practical, and the personal.

In addition we have woven stories throughout the collection as a hedge against becoming "high-minded" in our discussion. Hopefully these personal anecdotes will remind us that, while we may be able to articulate the dilemmas facing professionals, we have not settled them. We want these stories to be a safeguard against our theorizing the issues away from "real life" into the safety zones of abstraction.

We hope this book will provide a forum for dialogue among both professionals and nonprofessionals. If it provides occasion for professionals to reflect on their own professional journeys, if it creates a setting for conversation between professionals and nonprofessionals, if it allows nonprofessionals to listen in on professionals reflecting about their worlds, if it makes all of us more aware of the perils of professionalization, then the effort will have met our expectations.

We have focused attention on the process and consequences of professionalization. We are convinced that at the bottom of the professional drama is the issue of social power. (Perhaps it would be better to speak of the powerful and the powerless rather than the professional and nonprofessional.) We are contending here with how certain people and occupational groups become powerful. And we are curious about what that does to their identity, their values, their social relationships, their church life, and their faith.

There is a sense in which the following pieces represent the collective wisdom of a community of people on a journey from the plow to professions. With a few exceptions, the contributors write from the context of one of the major Mennonite denominations. As we edited, we were struck by the frequent references to the farm. The last three decades have resulted in a rapid move in the Mennonite community from the land to the office—an abrupt shift from field to profession—typically bypassing the factory and many blue collar jobs. Many Mennonites today discover that they are first-generation professionals. There have been some Mennonite professionals in the past, but the widespread influx into professions is a new and novel experience for a sizable group of Mennonites.

Working as newcomers in the world of professionalism raises provocative questions and creates dilemmas unknown in an agrarian culture. The first and second generations in any venture struggle to adapt their history and past tradition to the new setting. The clash of old and new, familiar and strange, produces a creative tension and experience. Such moments of social transition stimulate critical reflection.

Although the questions and essays in this collection are framed in the context of the Mennonite experience in professions, they are nevertheless enduring issues that will not fade or ought not wane for succeeding generations of professionals. Thus, we believe that the ideas and suggestions which follow will be useful and relevant to both those within and without the Mennonite community and to first-generation professionals as well as older professionals.

There is an ambivalence toward professions within the Anabaptist tradition of faith. On the one hand professionalism is strewn with the terms service, justice, help, and care—all virtues in this tradition. The chance to work and do good and be paid well all at once is welcomed as a chance to have one's religious cake and eat it, too. Those professions whose primary goal is to serve the public good are eagerly embraced.

On the other hand there is uneasiness about jumping on the professional bandwagon. Although the jargon and rhetoric sound good, there is the judgment that the major professions are at the very heart of social structure, that they stand at the very center of the "world." There is a fear that professions are not as serving as they claim to be, that they quickly become masters in disguise controlling the society, dominating other occupational groups, enslaving their own members, and caring less than completely about the public good. This collection finds itself in this second stream of thought—a bit uneasy, sometimes critical, not fully convinced about the merits of professions.

There are four relationships of professionalism which clarify the focus of this study. There is a macro relationship between *professions and the larger society.* This directs us to questions about the amount of influence professions have in the society at large and how they are nested in society's structure. Second, we can look at the link between the *profession and the professional.* Here the focus is on the manner in which professions select, train, control, and influence their members. At this level we can also inquire about the extent of a professional's loyalty, commitment, and involvement in the profession. A third bond involves the tie between the *professional and the client*. Here we are curious about the quality and amount of interaction, service, and distance in the relationship. Such a focus alerts us to questions regarding the abuse of power by either party. Finally, we can investigate the tie between the *professional and the church*. Does the church have any influence and relevance for the professional? How does someone's status in a profession alter their involvement in the life of a local congregation?

The chief peril, sometimes hidden and other times obvious throughout many of the pages of this book, is that professions have an uncanny tendency to subvert their original good intentions. We believe that at all four levels of analysis there is the likelihood of a subtle shift from a servant relationship to one of domination. Professions, while intending to serve the public good, are inclined to shape and form civil opinion, regulations, and behavior toward their own vested interests. Professions, while meaning to provide the tools for their members to serve, have a persistent proclivity to dominate and control their members and to protect the vested interests of the profession. Professionals who want to serve their clients' best interests may instead end up serving the profession. Professionals who desire to serve the church may find themselves professionalizing the church and dominating its decision-making process. There is the danger that at all four levels well-intentioned servants tend to turn into dominating masters.

Welcome to the conversation!

Donald B. Kraybill
Elizabethtown, Pennsylvania

Phyllis Pellman Good
Lancaster, Pennsylvania

The Process of Professionalization

CHAPTER ONE

The Professionalization of Everything and Everyone

By Donald B. Kraybill

The Magic Tag

"Professional" is the magic word that holds modern societies spellbound. The tag of professional is slapped on everything and on everyone. A friend recently started a part-time chimney sweeping business and printed up elegant business cards with the words "professional and courteous service" across the top. When asked about the "professional service," he grinned and said, "Well, I really haven't cleaned out any yet, but I thought the word professional would make it sound like I knew what I was doing." A television commercial for a bank tells us to "see a full service bank for 'professional answers.' " A piece of junk mail advertises professional lawn service. A local mortician promotes his services with the words, "We're the funeral professionals." In the want-ads I discover that I can have "professional window and carpet cleaning" done in my home. Another blurb tells me to be certain to contact a "fencing professional" if I'm building a fence in the yard.

And then I read that there is "professional service" for all my floral needs. Apparently I need flowers and can acquire them in a professional way. Unbelievably as I write these lines my daughter and her seven-year-old playmate walk in (without knocking) and plop a bouquet of day lilies on my desk. "Dad, we got them out in the weeds beside the burned-out barn (giggle,

giggle)." Unordered, unpaid for, improperly cut, and poorly arranged, but a spontaneous message of love sixteen days after Father's Day.

Another ad in the newspaper informs me that there's a "professional popcorn popper" which comes in a gift package "with professionally prepared corn and professional butter"—probably from professional cows with professional udders. While such careless and flippant use of the term "professional" evaporates its meaning, it still carries a strong appeal for most of us. The meaning of the word has been utterly corrupted, yet the professional label continues to be attractive, prestigious, and sought after.

Muddy Definitions

So what is a profession and who is a professional? I assumed that any decent scholarly text could tell me if realtors, sanitary engineers, truck drivers, and medical technicians were professionals. But dozens of scholarly articles later, I'm convinced they can't. There is agreement that physicians, professors, lawyers, and ministers ("professional" ones at least) are professionals, but beyond that the conceptual water gets very muddy. There are lists and lists of different traits used to define a profession, usually including:

- extensive training and education;
- specialized knowledge which is both technical and abstract;
- rigorous standards for admission and practice;
- a high degree of internalized self-control;
- an orientation to serving the public good;
- legal recognition through forms of licensure and certification;
- membership in and control by a professional organization.

Each scholar adds his own pet trait and the lists get longer and longer.

When I asked some friends how they would define a professional, I heard: "They do white collar work instead of blue collar work." "Professionals work with their heads instead of their hands." "They get paid for what they do; they're not amateurs or volunteers." "Professionals don't have regular old jobs." "They are very trained and skilled in an area." But these typical distinctions are not much help if we want to know if a Certified Public Accountant is a professional or not. Since the term professional carries such a strong social appeal, the pressure is on to find a definition broad enough so that almost everyone can slip into the professional ball park.

Three Definitions

Social scientists have often used three approaches in defining a profession: (1) The *trait* approach involves the conceptual development of a set of traits and then matches the real social characteristics of a particular profession with the abstract model. (2) The *consensus* approach says that if an occupation has been labeled a profession and if most of society think of it as a profession, then it should be regarded as a profession regardless of whether or not it fits a list of traits. (3) And finally, the *ask-the-natives* approach suggests that one simply asks the persons employed in an occupation if they consider themselves professionals. If they do think of themselves as professionals, they will tend to emulate whatever society considers "professional" behavior and their occupation should be tagged a profession.

The *trait* approach is the most common, although there is little agreement on which traits should be used. The *ask-the-natives* approach is so broad that it virtually allows anyone to walk through the professional door. There is a fourth approach which I think is the most useful in clarifying the nature of professions. This model doesn't neatly sort occupations into professional and unprofessional niches, but rather looks at the degree to which an occupation is a profession in terms of its social power.

Monopoly and Dominance

The *power* approach does not focus on the type of work or the length of training required, but concentrates on the extent to which an occupation can *control* the nature of its work and can control other occupations. Freidson (1977) says professionals "have the ability and organizational power to control themselves, the terms, conditions, and content of their work." In other words, a profession is an occupational organization that gains for its members a monopoly on a particular segment of the labor market. When a profession achieves a monopoly, it controls who gets in, how they're trained, how they work, who they work for, under what type of public regulations they work, and how much they are paid.

In addition to a profession developing a monopoly, it tries to free itself from the dominance of other organizations and, in turn, to control the work of other occupational groups. From the power perspective, *monopoly* and *dominance* become the key yardsticks to judge the extent to which an occupation has grown up into a profession. This method is not a neat scheme for sorting occupations into professional and unprofessional boxes. Occupations can be sorted along a continuum of professionalism by the extent to which they control the conditions of their work and are free of control by other occupational groups. Ivan Illich (1977:17), a critic of the professions, says that the mark of a professional is not "income, long training, delicate tasks, or social standing ... rather it is his authority to define a person as client, to determine that person's need, and to hand the person a prescription."

Two examples illustrate the power perspective. When I was on a sabbatical leave from college teaching, I worked as a laborer in a factory. I had virtually no control over any other occupational groups. The workers scored zero on monopoly and on dominance. In contrast, when I am teaching I have a great deal of control over the content and conditions of my work. Individually and as an occupational group, faculty have some control over other occupational groups: secretaries, student assistants, paraprofessionals, librarians, janitors. More importantly teachers control the ideas introduced into their classrooms. Thus, in terms of monopoly and dominance, a professor is much more professionalized than a factory worker.

A less obvious example is the distinction between physicians and pharmacists. Both are considered professionals; both have technical skills which require extensive training; and both have licenses which give them a monopoly over their work. But as Freidson (1977) points out, there is a critical difference: the pharmacist can only work at the order of the physician. Physicians, in addition to monopolizing their work with controls over recruitment, practice, and licensure, also dominate other occupational groups. They have supervisory power over an increasing number of technicians, pharmacists, and paraprofessionals who cannot work without the authorization of a physician and whose products, like a lab test, are only usable by physicians. In this sense physicians are much more professionalized than pharmacists.

The power perspective, then, asks how an occupational group controls the general public, government regulations, other professions, economic organizations, their own members, and their clients. Answers to such questions permit us to compare occupational groups as to their degree of professionalization.

The Profession as a Team

At the bottom of the professional process is membership in a community of other professionals. Illich (1977) highlights the membership question with his observation that morticians formed a profession when they acquired the muscle to have the police stop burials not in their control. A profession is not merely a tag tacked on one's job; it is a social group with enormous influence and power over its members. When reflecting upon the professional experience it is easy to be trapped into thinking about a solitary professional doing his or her "professional" work in an isolated office with a single client or patient. Slipping into this rut of individual analysis neglects the fact that the professional is a member of a team which is playing a game. There are rules, positions, referees, and umpires officiating the game, many times out of sight. Or to use the image of the stage, the professional is an actor along with others who are staging a performance. There are scripts to follow, makeup to put on, costumes to wear, directors to follow, and audiences to worry about. There is a front stage where protocol dictates functions and there is a back stage where the real structure of the drama is revealed.

Professionals must be seen as products of a social subculture and as members of organizational teams. The professional subculture or community is greater than the sum of its individual members. It has a life of its own. Its ethos, influence, and momentum make it a powerful force in the life of its members. As a social unit the profession becomes concerned about perpetuating

---

Why Professionalism Makes Me Uneasy

By Lois Y. Kenagy

As Mennonites have increasingly accepted American middle-class values, we have tended to adopt an attitude of awe toward those who have achieved professional status in our communities. For many years we have seen ourselves as the quiet of the land and often as unworthy or inferior people. Now, when one of our number achieves professional status and receives recognition in the larger society, we are quite proud.

The special status granted to professionals in the community tends to be carried over into the church. For instance, one church-related board as recently as 1976 asked that persons nominated be chosen from the categories of "church person, businessperson, educator, and *professional*." Professionals included "doctors, attorneys, and others who have specialized resources and technical knowledge which persons in the other categories cannot provide." Consequently, that particular board included several doctors, although medical expertise was not related to work at hand. Medical experience, in my opinion, did not provide better qualifications for the work of that board than the vocational experiences of a farmer, electrician, welder, housewife, or nurse. Did the board merely want the influence of the doctor's wealth or community status?

Why am I uneasy about professionalism? I wish there were no such term. Why is a secretary

itself and protecting its turf from other encroaching professions. It champions its vested interests and tries to gain additional advantage for its members.

There are numerous ways in which a profession influences its players and actors. There are formal codes and regulations to follow, certification exams to pass, in-service courses to take, and disciplinary actions for inappropriate conduct. But even more significant are the subtle and less tangible modes of control. In the training process a profession teaches its members how to think about the world. It constructs and transmits a world-view or an ideology. This includes not only learning about the virtues of the profession, but also about the pitfalls of other competing

---

just an office employee but a lawyer a professional? an elementary teacher just a teacher, but a teacher of college students a professional? a nurse just an employee but a doctor a professional? The nomenclature would be unimportant if it did not give special status or recognition to persons termed professional. It's the status that troubles me.

What do I do with my uneasiness about professionalism? First, I must search my own soul with honesty and openness to ferret out any seeds of jealousy. Too long I have been in awe of intellectual and academic achievement. Is it smugness I feel when asked what kind of profession I'm in and I answer, "I'm a farmer's wife, a mother, and a church and community volunteer"? Or is it honest satisfaction that I no longer need to be ashamed of not being a "professional" because my gifts are being utilized in the church without professional status?

The kingdom of God needs all of us: housewives, farmers, nurses, teachers, students, cleaning women, miners, carpenters, businessmen, secretaries, as well as all the professionals. The gifts of all our members need to be developed for the work of the kingdom. The pecking order so common in the animal kingdom is inappropriate in the new community of believers. Insofar as professionalism contributes to such a pecking order, it subverts the nature of God's new community, the church.

professions. Such ingroup thinking is hard to shake off—it tends to stick. As a sociologist I still find myself writing long paragraphs on the necessity of seeing persons as members of social groups!

A profession teaches its members how to think about clients, the general public, government, and economics. Even though these topics may not be officially covered in Sales 101 (Introduction to Real Estate Transactions), these values are passed on through off-the-cuff discussions at coffee breaks and parties. In mature professional life, the professional is a member of a social network of other professionals which subtly spells out how to create and maintain a professional image—what kind of car, furniture, vacation, subscription, suit, and opinions are necessary to project a professional image.

I was amazed some years ago when a colleague, who was lecturing to a group of fifty persons, pointed out the one physician in the group and said, "I can pick them out every time." Professionals who don't follow these informal expectations are punished with ridicule, gossip, and the stigmatized tag of being "unprofessional." The high social cost of deviance from these norms and values assures compliance and conformity. The profession becomes an emotional home for the professional, serving as a reference group that determines values and provides standards for ethical conduct. It serves as a powerful point of reference which the individual member uses to determine his or her success and achievement. In this way, it is an influential shaper of self-image and a motivator of behavior.

The Mythology of Professionalism

There is a widespread set of attitudes, beliefs, and assumptions about professionals subscribed to by professionals and nonprofessionals alike, a "mythology" based on a mixture of fact and fiction. This conglomeration of beliefs about professionals is deemed necessary, for it grants authority to professionals and convinces nonprofessionals to allow professionals the right to exercise that power. For example, I will permit my dentist to poke around in my mouth only if I believe she "knows what she's doing," and if I trust her to make correct judgments. I must believe in and trust her ability before I am willing to open my mouth. There is an ambivalence in this mythology of professionalism—a love/hate, trust/mistrust complex. Professionals are respected, admired, and emulated; at the same time they are suspect, ridiculed, and castigated. I asked a group of college freshmen for their opinions on professionals and received the following comments which demonstrate this ambivalence:

> "They should be right because they are supposed to know what they are talking about."

> "They are on a pedestal, placed above the rest of society, because they are 'more than human.' "

> "They are out to hurt people by cheating."

> "They are flawless and looked up to."

> "They were probably lucky to be rich from the beginning and most likely male."

> "They probably have some brains but their ethics are questionable."

> "Professionals are smarter than the average, make more money, and have respect and trust in their decisions."

> "They know it all, sit at desks, and have jobs above the regular working class."

> "They are rich, have everything they want, and have no worries."

> "Professionals are polished, wealthy, and very fortunate to be where they are."

> "They are good, know best, and make a lot of money."

> "They are distinguished, very learned, and stuck on themselves."

> "They are rich and rip off the public."

"Professionals have good jobs, are special people, know how to handle people, and know what they're doing."

"They are rich, intelligent, sometimes crooked and snobbish."

"They can be trusted; they are good people."

"They are respected sometimes in their field and out of their field."

John McKinlay (1979) points out that one of the central elements in this mythology of professionalism is that professionals are believed to be qualitatively different from nonprofessionals. It is said that professionals are more honest, dedicated, concerned, service-oriented, competent, and caring.

It may be that professionals are taught to do their work in careful and competent ways, but that doesn't mean that professionals are *always* better than nonprofessionals. Any alert observer knows that student assistants are often better teachers than professors, that physicians' assistants can care for patients as well or better than physicians, and that neighborly chatting is sometimes more effective than sophisticated therapy. There is ample empirical evidence to demonstrate that the paraprofessionals and others who work under a professional's supervision are often more effective and careful practitioners than their bosses. And we all know that there are some very caring and compassionate electricians and janitors.

A second aspect of the creed of professionalism is that "professionals ought to be trusted." McKinlay (1979) says the motto of the professions is "let the taker believe in us." Trust in professionals is widely accepted in Western culture and is necessary for much professional practice. Without trust, I won't submit myself to the care of a physician. It is believed that professionals ought to be trusted because:

- they have special training and knowledge;
- they have been specially called to their profession by a higher authority;
- they are committed to the high ideals of altruism and public service;
- they are selflessly concerned about the welfare of those they serve.

The less knowledgeable and the more needy the client, the more he or she must blindly trust the professional.

This mythology, though necessary, carries dangers. It is possible that the lay public will actually believe the mythology and be afraid to critique, evaluate, or question professional practice. The public may blindly follow expert advice and refuse to exercise their own judgment and discretion. On the other side, the professionals may also believe the mythology and belittle the efforts and opinions of the less informed. The professionals' temptation is to use and abuse the mythology to protect and advance their own vested interests.

Professional Appeal

The widespread pursuit of "professional jobs instead of regular jobs"; the application of the professional label to all kinds of work and service; the flattery obtained by calling jobs professional; and the sales advantage gained by tagging products professional—all of these facts are evidence that the word "professional" carries a great deal of social power. Even though the term has been applied to everything, it seems not to have lost its social muscle. Even its occasional mistrust and derision is evidence of its power. The social weight and meaning of the term is far more significant than its technical use in distinguishing occupations. In boldest terms, the word professional means power. It means the power:

- to engender respect and status;
- to develop a monopoly over work;
- to determine needs and prescriptions;
- to supervise and control other occupations;
- to expect trust;
- to work with freedom and autonomy;
- to set fees and charges;
- to establish the rules of work;
- to control secret knowledge;
- to use influential symbols and titles;
- to generate a secure income;
- to avoid public review and evaluation.

Because it means all of this, the professional appeal will continue, the mythology of professionalism will survive, and the possibility of abuse will not fade.

CHAPTER TWO

On Becoming a Professional

By Ruth Detweiler Lesher

White Rats and Christian Service

Since I grew up as a Mennonite farm girl, I was accustomed to animals when I began experimenting with a special breed of white rats in the Eastern Mennonite College psychology department. By better understanding the harmful effects of a particular chemical on rats, I hoped to contribute to the improvement of the health of migrant workers whose skin was exposed to large amounts of this chemical as they picked fruits and vegetables. This seemed politically and socially relevant and carried the promise of improving the health care of an oppressed and impoverished group of persons.

Soon I learned that if I wanted to continue studying human behavior, the appropriate next step was to earn a PhD in psychology. So I began pursuing that goal. But I did wonder if that course might separate me from those I wanted to serve. Would I lose sight of real need in the process? The power and status that society bequeaths to a PhD was almost embarrassing.

I also wondered if my going to school to become more powerful and more effective in meeting the needs of our society was just a myth, a rationalization, a twentieth-century brainwashing. What about the Anabaptist style of witness in the world that discourages participation in the system that it wishes to change? Would I change so much as I became a professional that

I'd no longer elicit trust from those with whom I wanted to work and live? Would I ultimately end up studying the phenomenon of footwashing—the effects on the washer and the washed—without ever washing someone's feet?

PhDs and Husbands

I thought that if men didn't want women to have careers, they probably wouldn't marry those who went to graduate school. I also was afraid that if a man found me attractive enough for marriage, he probably wouldn't want me to attend graduate school. Not only did I believe men felt that way; I also doubted that I could really be a good wife and mother if I was determined to do further study in psychology.

After deciding to begin graduate studies, I soon faced the possibility of marriage. I felt that I had to choose one or the other. A good marital relationship was important to me. I thought it would be safer to go to graduate school first; then get married. But I was afraid that if I did that I wouldn't have as many opportunities to get married. And I didn't want to bother with dating while I was concentrating all my energies in my graduate work in psychology.

Before entering graduate school I realized that a good marital relationship was more important to me than a PhD. And a good relationship turned into a marriage. My husband saw no reason why I couldn't pursue my professional goals while we were married. But I was still uncertain as to how it would really work out. I wanted to go to school on the West Coast so I could study both theology and psychology. But I didn't want to drag someone else there since it was a six-year program. I sat on my dreams for a short while, got some work experience, and had a chance to enjoy married life.

I was quite surprised one evening to come home from work and learn that my husband sensed that God was leading us to Fuller Theological Seminary, the school that I wanted to attend. Neither of us was accustomed to receiving such clear responses to prayer. And I had seldom heard of situations in which a husband sensed the call for him and his wife to do something which was so liberating for the wife. We had often wished for this kind of clarity when discerning God's will before. I was not called alone to pursue graduate school; and my husband did not drag me into "his calling." The Lord called us individually and together.

Ivory Towers in Urban Poverty

On our wedding trip my husband and I visited several Christian communities and were impressed with the rich and full life that evolves from such single-minded commitment to Christ and to others. Perhaps we were giving too much priority to success in our career and neglecting our calling to the body of

---

Becoming a Professional Accountant
Some Anonymous Observations

In my first days working for one of the "Big Eight" national accounting firms, I quickly discovered some specific things I was expected to do to project the image of a "professional accountant." I was explicitly told some of these rules for professional image creation. Other orders were more subtle, but very real if I hoped to "make it professionally."

Proper dress included:
- shoes could not be scuffed;
- no clothing purchased at Sears; such outfits were too cheap and common;
- hair cuts were advised frequently; once, I was instructed to get it cut.

Accessories:
- a "Cross" pen was required—BIC's and Paper Mates looked unprofessional;
- a $140 leather brief case was a must;
- an American Express card or Diners Club card was necessary and carried more respect than the common man's version: Master Card and VISA;
- a "top of the line" car that was "loaded" was useful; a bottom of the line Rabbit or Chevette was a detriment.

Food:
- we were taught to never eat at McDonalds with a client;
- it was preferable to buy wine

Christ. Should we participate in a community before professional school? we asked. Then, if God calls us from that to further study, our priority and our base for ministry would be established. Part of our affirmation that God was calling us both directly to graduate school came when we received an invitation to join a household of students interested in Christian com-

---

rather than beer for clients; beer is the working man's drink;

• it was permissible to take a client to a Steak House for lunch as long as one did not buy "only salad" or the "working man's special."

Service:

• we were urged to donate blood to the Red Cross and to prominently display our donation card on top of our packet of credit cards;

• it was advisable to "ride" a service club like the Jaycees in order to keep up our "service" image in the community;

• contributions to the United Way were expected so that our firm could maintain a good image. The United Way contribution was a kind of tax to "keep the natives in place," so that minorities could not push our firm around too much.

Lifestyle:

• there was a good deal of pressure to join a tennis or racquet club; golf and country clubs were archaic;

• it was an asset to have a wife who "knew the arts" but not one who was an elementary teacher;

• expensive vacations to Las

Vegas, Bermuda, or Europe were biannual expectations;

• we were expected to attend the Friday night office parties at the home of one of the bosses;

• owning a nice house in the "right neighborhood" helped a lot;

• being an active Republican and attending the local symphony were distinct assets.

Attitudes:

• accountants are the *best* professionals: they are not emotional, like lawyers, or just glorified technicians, like doctors;

• accountants are also better than teachers because teachers have to have unions in order to get a contract;

• professional accountants socialize with other professionals in the office, but socializing with the support staff—secretaries, clerks, bookkeepers, and maintenance— was kept to a minimum;

• our offices were on the 24th floor so we could really "look down on things"—we were "on top" of everything.

I have struggled with how to relate these expectations with my understanding of the demands of Christ in my life.

munity. It is with this group that we still find Christian fellowship and accountability to other persons.

In four of our five years in Pasadena, we have been able to participate in our local community and have been deeply involved with the church. We completed three years as program directors of a Voluntary Service program, a good way to get outside of the ivory tower mentality. I live in two worlds, one of professional academicians and another one of searching VSers and illiterate adult neighbors. Our Voluntary Service unit is located in a very poor urban area that is shifting from a largely black to a Mexican population. This local world has been good for me because it provides an utterly different world-view than the one taken for granted in professional psychology. I have a counter perspective for critically evaluating some platitudes alive in the psychological ivory tower.

Fed Up with Living Simply

Spending five years on a student budget has made me less appreciative of simple lifestyles. But it has helped me to better identify with those who don't choose to be poor. The longer I live on a student budget, the less it is something that I want to choose. The longer I have to live simply, the more I find myself making choices which I once thought were foolish for someone with a limited budget. For example, my choice to skip a meal so that I can go to a concert or to a restaurant for dessert is really not much different from my neighbor's decision to buy a soda and corn chips instead of fruit. Enjoying something special becomes as "essential" as buying items that are usually considered necessities. I now understand how junk food becomes an occasional "necessity," and how one new fancy dress may get selected over three nice used ones.

On the other hand, my poverty is temporary. I have chosen to live this way so that I can make a large educational investment and live on a larger income in the future. My neighbors' budgets, however, won't increase. They are not growing in personal status and power like I am. So I never really come close to the nature of poverty around me, the inability to choose.

My dilemma is this: In the process of gaining power, status, and earning potential, I have grown weary of feeling poor. Being able to purchase nice things has grown in importance for me. At the moment when I will be able to deliberately choose a simple lifestyle, but have the means to do otherwise, I find myself less willing to live simply.

Farmers and Professionals

My husband and I grew up around farms. I don't know how we'll resolve our strong desire to be on a farm. For the first three years of graduate school, my husband almost decided each year to farm instead of becoming a professional. And we still wonder if we can be professionals and give up the farm.

On the farm I learned to make decisions and to take the initiative when tasks needed to be done. Herding cattle and gathering eggs were never predictable experiences. Such jobs are not easily outlined and executed. Within the general plan, one has to learn the right time for each move and be prepared for unexpected animal behavior. Farming also taught me how to work hard. I knew that certain tasks had to be finished before sundown or before the thunderstorm.

Autonomy, freedom, individual initiative, and the need for quick decisions make the responsibilities of a farmer and a professional similar in many ways. Both involve risk and reward. The freedom to "be one's own boss" is similar in the stable and the office. The decisions in both occupations are made against equally unpredictable odds of changing weather, changing human emotions, behaviors, and money markets. And yet there is a profound difference between life on the land and life at the desk. Historically, the farmer had little power over people compared to the professional of today. The farmer did not enjoy the prestigious respect given to the professional.

As a Christian and a Mennonite, I cringe when I'm told I'm powerful. I have a string of negative associations with that word: power, powerless, oppression, political manipulation, war, kill-ing, personal aggression, domination, institutions. What does a Mennonite farmer do with his power? Why does farming appear at first to be such a humble task? What is the difference between power over the beasts and the earth, and the power a professional has over other people?

My tradition didn't teach me how to handle power. Quiet farming was such an easy way to salt the earth and light the world. The professional world demands vocal, aggressive, and shrewd power brokers to cope with the multiplicity of forces in professional life. This seems so different from my cultural heros—the quiet, faithful farmers.

Being a Christian woman doesn't make power easier to handle. Differences between a Mennonite farm woman and a professional woman have more to do with the status that society gives educational degrees than with a shift from stereotyped feminine skills to masculine ones. Many Mennonite women that I've observed on the farm demonstrate significant responsibility, independence, and good management skills.

The farm is not without sexism, but I have seldom observed women waiting for their husbands to tell them when and how to manage the freezing and canning process or the quilting designs. Rather, I often find each spouse with autonomous spheres of responsibility. The women usually have meals and children on their list. Husbands may give final authority on certain matters. But this also happens without mutual consent when husbands and wives are both professionals.

I am not totally at peace with the realization that it probably won't be my garden or my quilts that will be my most admired contributions. Sometimes an acknowledgment of my professional status feels out of character as if I'd been complimented on my wheat crop this year. (My growing professional status as a woman is about as unexpected and unbelievable as a woman growing wheat.)

I am grateful for the models of my mother and other Christian women who demonstrate good management, independence, and perseverence. However, among Mennonite women there is a scarcity of females who have attained societal status, who have the power that comes with a PhD or a law degree. I wonder how owning this status will affect my ability to model Christian servanthood. How will I handle the honor associated with the PhD as a woman in a man's professional world and as a Christian woman who believes in the power of servanthood? Will I know when to stop climbing? As I work with people instead of rats and chickens, will the internalized convictions of my tradition be strong enough to tarnish the appeal of professionalism?

CHAPTER THREE

Second Thoughts About a PhD

By Carl Bowman

Graduate School or Turkey Factory

As the end of each semester approaches, I ardently heave term papers, final exams, and methodological masterpieces of statistical wizardry over the stern of the ship, hoping to lighten the load before the vessel capsizes in a sea of deadlines. Twice a year, during much troubled and stormy times, the perennial question inevitably arises in my mind: "Is this really better than the turkey factory?" (I've worked in one for several summers.) Although the question seems simple, it is really more serious than one might imagine, for education at the graduate level is always a matter of choice. Long ago I mastered the fundamentals which all persons must learn; each semester I must decide anew whether the pressure of academic competition, the mounds of paper work, and the twelve-hour workdays are truly worth that professional position which looms four years down the road (if I'm lucky) or that extra bit of status assigned to the return address label, "Joe S. Smart, PhD." Why do I continue on? Will the pure enjoyment of the professional position really exceed the personal satisfaction of refinishing an old piece of oak furniture as an antique dealer? Is a flexible work schedule and the independence of professionalism really worth the anxiety of knowing one's work is never done? I really wonder about such questions.

It's a safe bet that social status propels many graduate students to spend twenty-two of their first twenty-seven years of life in school. No matter how radical we graduate students profess to be, no matter how much we can see through the facades of the "establishment," there's little doubt that we will all warm up inside when we see in print the title "Bob Bright, MS" or "Sarah Toosmart, PhD." After all, during the graduate school journey, students quickly learn to be sensitive to credentials. For instance, when a student hears a profound, original statement uttered by a total stranger, it becomes vital to question a friend regarding the "profess-or's" academic background before evaluating the remark. If a stranger is a PhD from Yale, one nods in silent agreement. If he or she has an MA from Indiana University, one might argue the point. If, however, the stranger has a BA from Lord Fairfax Community College, or merely a high school diploma from Buffalo Gap High, one knowingly smirks under one's breath and pays attention to more worthy individuals. The response strategy is based on the titles, not on the content of the initial statement. Students learn this early; they discover that this "Golden Rule of Credibility" will guide their future acquaintances in judging their own opinions on important matters.

Family pressure also prods many of us to stay in school. At the graduate level the pressure is more covert than overt, but this makes it no less real. Everyone knows parents love to talk about their "son at Harvard Law School" or their "daughter, the psychologist." Nothing brings more joy than revealing that "Georgie, Jr.," has received another degree and will be guest lecturer at a consortium of universities in the fall. What is true for parents is also true for in-laws, only their pressure can be even more intimidating because theirs isn't the unconditional love expected from parents. A student who cranks out the final paper of the semester, and makes the brave decision to escape the hectic pace by leaving the ivory towers behind forever without a degree in hand, risks being stigmatized for life. How does one explain to family members that painting houses is more fun than writing papers? Does it make any difference that a budding scholar loves tuning up Volkswagens? If this is the case, isn't staying in school being dishonest with oneself? Alas, these considerations are often beyond the comprehension of one's family. Fathers, ministers, fathers-in-law, and former professors all know that dropping out of school is bad. To them it's very simple: A degree equals success and no degree means failure.

If it's true that the students who "make it" in graduate school are often the most ambitious status seekers or the most aggressive "dollar chasers," the ones who hope to eventually move in "all the right circles" and achieve a lucrative lifestyle, then perhaps the student who drops out is merely refusing to join the high-society rat race.

In this world of twisted values, what is "success"? Perhaps the individual who drops out of school in spite of family pressures, and drops in to a more satisfying pursuit is, in fact, "the successful" one. Aren't those who let others determine their life's course, while remaining untrue to themselves, the real "failures"? Might staying in school sometimes be equivalent to failure? In the realm of idealism, the answer is probably "yes." However, in the realm of contemporary society, unfortunately, "success" is still measured in terms of occupational prestige, level of income, and educational degrees. In light of this reality, students keep signing up semester after semester.

And so, these external motivators (status, family pressure, potential financial rewards) and personal motivations (such as the desire to make a real impact upon the world, to humanize an often inhumane society, and sometimes the pure delight of learning) keep me in school in pursuit of the graduate degree. Hopefully if this degree means little else, it will confer a certain legitimacy upon my ideas so that my desire to accomplish or change certain things in life will seem credible, even if unrealistic.

Given my decision (for the moment, anyway) to remain in school, certain aspects of graduate study—indeed, of professionalism in general—stand out in my mind as being ironic, or even paradoxical.

On Being the Expert

All through my life I have been the student, the apprentice, the bright young chap eager to *learn* about the world and *receive* the wisdom and knowledge of other, more skilled individuals. Now all of a sudden, as a PhD student at the University of Wisconsin, I occasionally find myself in the position where I am supposed to be the expert—I am the one who "knows." When I find myself in this role, I want to shout: Wait a minute! What's going on here? Who am I kidding? To know that it is *not* my extensive knowledge which makes me the "expert" in these situations, but rather my prestige as a graduate student in one of the top sociology departments in the nation, makes me feel like I'm playing in some grand game. It seems so arbitrary.

The incongruity of this situation hit me while I was in an airplane over Chicago, Illinois, on my way to a five-day stay in Ann Arbor, Michigan. In Ann Arbor, I was to serve as a visiting research consultant on a project sponsored by the Institute for Social Research (ISR) of the University of Michigan. I sat on the plane in my shirt sleeves and blue jeans, opposite others in three-piece suits. As I pulled papers from my yellow backpack, they opened their leather attache cases. I thought again to myself, "Who am I kidding?" It seemed so incomprehensible that my flight, limousine service, hotel, and meals were being paid for by my "company" (as I knew was the case with my fellow travelers). What was it that had suddenly transformed me from a lowly "learner" into a traveling "professional"? Certainly it was neither my increased knowledge nor my breadth of experience. It was simply my new "professional passport" as a doctoral student at the University of Wisconsin.

Upon arriving at the ISR (that's another sign of professionalism—one quickly learns to abbreviate things so only in-group members of the trade will understand), I began working with an advanced student about two years my senior. He was to be my computer technician—the one who would make the technical changes in a data set which I and other professionals hoped to use. (Professionally, this is known as "data cleaning.")

This hierarchy of positions seemed totally ironic and I felt I was being pretentious: here I was, the BA from a tiny, rural college doing the "think work," while my colleague, an MA from the prestigious University of Michigan, was following my orders. Although I had scarcely more training in research techniques than my MA co-worker, I realized that I had to think of myself as the PhD student in sociology and play the role of a rigorous, scientific professional. My colleague was merely trained in the soft discipline of social work and, therefore, was less qualified. All these new rules seemed arbitrary and somewhat ludicrous to me, but I had to swallow my humility and accept the new roles as defined.

Technique and Ethics

Why pursue sociology at the graduate level? Apart from the external pressures already touched upon, I hoped to understand the dynamics which drive society so that someday I might help correct some of the abuses which are rampant in the world. I was motivated in part by concerns from my Church of the Brethren roots. I wanted to understand the undue emphasis our society places upon the individual (as opposed to the group), social prestige, material gain and reward, and finally, military power. By studying these issues, I hoped to arrive at a clearer comprehension of how to combat them. This is the idealism with which I first approached graduate studies.

Sadly, from the very start, graduate study was an exercise in disillusionment. My vague hope of wanting to understand human existence was slowly eroded by tables, numbers, and quantitative methods. I discovered, for instance, that one could do commendable research on Chicanos and Chicano oppression without ever meeting a Chicano or traveling to the Southwest. Moreover, you don't even have to speak their language! You merely need to understand numbers and statistical methods. While I wanted to learn about society through humanistically oriented courses in social history and philosophy, I discovered these were less pertinent than nativity figures, mortality rates, and demographic techniques. At first this seemed paradoxical, but gradually I came to accept the usefulness of some of these techniques. However, I am plagued by the question: Am I learning to tolerate valid scientific techniques? or am I being indoctrinated in truly sterile methods? Whatever the case, these "scientific" procedures for social analysis are clearly more marketable in our technical society than is some ill-defined familiarity with social history and philosophical ethics.

Ultimately, however, the technically competent professional must face the limits of his or her technical skills. He or she must integrate all those newly acquired professional skills with the idealistic concerns and passions which originally led to graduate study. Professional programming in graduate school often resists ethical questions and moral integration. If ethical concerns can't be integrated with technical training, might they be sacrificed for income, prestige, and domestic stability?

"Expressing the Stuff Right"

There is *substance* within every academic discipline: sociology, psychology, and biology all have a body of knowledge which the graduate student must master. And then there are *symbols:* the student must master not only the substance, but also the *language* of the discipline. It is as important to express the stuff right as it is to express the right stuff when interacting with fellow ivory tower residents. In graduate school substance is acquired formally, but the symbols are learned informally. Even though I haven't taken courses in the language of sociology, I learned the jargon all the same. Incorrect symbols, for example, often invalidate good substance; and well-chosen symbols, on the other hand, can often compensate for a lack of substance. Articulation is the name of the game. After all, our professional language is what distinguishes us from the person on the street. It acts as an ID tag which reads *Professional* in big, black letters. In fact, that's *all* our language says to most nonprofessionals, since they can't penetrate the code.

Ironically, language often becomes a barrier to communication. As a graduate student, one is no longer "flooded with

homework"; one is "inundated with assignments." Dropping-
out of graduate school is no longer "shameful"; it's "ignomi-
nious." Teachers aren't "terribly picky and boring"; they are
"perniciously pedantic."

As a sociology graduate student interested in social theory, I
was especially blessed with a wordy discipline. Among other
things I learned that:

> One must always strive to ascertain an author's metaphysical tenets
> and his working epistemology when critically analyzing one of his works.
> Once discerned, epistemology and metaphysical premises will be indica-
> tive of the weltanschaung which the author has implicitly adopted. Con-
> comitantly, one should also be able to identify the sociological paradigm
> which functions as the author's analytic foundation. These factors are all
> integral to the critical reading of seminal works in the field.

With command of such jargon, I've passed the "professional"
test. My newfound language is an effective *barrier* to communication. Now my discourse is confined to other esoteric intellectuals who can decode it.

The Graduate Student Mask

You ask me who I am? That's easy! I'm Carl Bowman from
the Shenandoah Valley in Virginia, the guy who subscribes to the
Brethren ethic of pacifism, community, and simplicity. And what
are my goals in life? Oh, maybe I'd like to teach at a *small*
college, interact meaningfully with a *small* group of students, and
do some high quality research (not necessarily empirical) at a
moderate pace. In such a setting I could develop my own understanding of issues which I find relevant, while at the same time
contribute to the academic and ethical development of students. I
might even have some time left to spend with my family. I don't
care for large doses of social prestige and I'm not terribly de-
sirous of a large salary, although I would like to own a modest
place in a semirural setting, and be free to travel occasionally.

But when Professor Edward Leet asks, Who are you? the
answer changes: "I'm Carl Bowman, PhD student in sociology.
Yes that's right, the bright young prospect from a school you've

never heard of in the East. Oh yes, I'm the one who served as substitute director of a small social research center as an undergraduate. You're right, that was an advantageous opportunity. It provided an excellent background in applied research and statistics, and sharpened my computer skills so that I wouldn't have to bother with such rudimentary learning at the graduate level. My professional goals? Well, Professor E. Leet, it's difficult to look ten years into the future. For the moment, my primary concern is to complete a review of Chicano literature, perform some preliminary data analyses, and in general, to progress as rapidly as possible on my thesis. Yes, I'm affiliated with the 'SEC,' 'Complex Org.,' 'Political Soc.,' and 'Rural Soc.' areas of the department. Maybe we can discuss funding prospects and the theory preliminary exam next week, in case this week doesn't suit, Professor E. Leet."

Realistically (now that Professor E. Leet is gone), I know at this point that I'll continue my studies at least through another academic year. Beyond that, it's anyone's guess. Although I wouldn't lie to Professor E. Leet about my plans, neither would I be totally forward. To do so—to indicate that my design is not to become a scholar of national reknown by publishing four articles a year—might destroy his interest in my development. His interest is to train young scholars who will go out and make a name for themselves, thereby enhancing his own prestige in the academic community. Most of my professors think that a Wisconsin-trained PhD teaching at a small college would be like "driving a Cadillac through a cornfield." There are certainly exceptions to this rule among the faculty. I may have exaggerated the "graduate student mask"; the exaggeration is intentional, however, for it contains important elements of "graduate school reality." Anyway, I must don my mask again and pull this script from the typewriter, for I hear Professor E. Leet coming down the hall.

CHAPTER FOUR

From Amish to Professional and Back Again

By Nancy Fisher Outley

An Amish Professional

Amish society is a community of nonprofessionals. However, many in the community have developed knowledge and skills that would qualify them as competent agriculturists and home economists. Most Amish are professionals in the sense that they have successfully mastered and competently practice a set of skills and techniques. If success is measured by outcome or results, surely Amish farms and the array of handicrafts and culinary goods within the home are evidence of the work of highly qualified "professional" people. But, our society has ruled that no matter how successful the outcome, it is only professional if an individual passes through a long academic process. Using our society's definition of professional, I had no professional role models as a young Amish child.

In the Amish community, education and professionalism are devalued. Humility is the highest value. Pursuing education propels one toward vanity, the opposite of humility. Vanity—thinking of oneself as better than others—interferes with brotherhood and community and is considered sinful. The pitfall of education is spelled out by the apostle Paul in 1 Corinthians 8:1: "Knowledge puffeth up." Since I had no professional role models, it is unusual that I had such a strong inner desire to continue my education beyond the eighth grade. My immediate environment did have a great deal of unusual educational stimuli: numerous contacts with outsiders, exposure to other lifestyles, books and magazines, periodic non-Amish boarders who lived with us; in one case this meant exposure to the Sunday newspaper and access to the Sunday comic section; I also took trips to New York City and the beach with non-Amish friends.

Very early in my childhood my emotional antennae picked up attitudes of respect from outsiders as they related to my parents. During summer days my mother would load my express wagon with the overabundance of our garden, some freshly dressed chickens, and eggs, which she and I pulled through town to peddle. In that situation my mother may have appeared to be in a role of low status. However, she related to others as an equal and received respect in return. In retrospect, I think that because of her strong work ethic, my mother could not justify stopping by someone's house for a cup of tea, so she devised peddling as a means to socialize with others. I remember thoroughly enjoying the excursions, listening to my mother discuss an array of issues with her customers and friends. When I became older I assumed the responsibility of peddling produce on my own to form my own independent relationships with the townpeople.

My father, in a much quieter manner, established very positive relationships in the wider community. Early in my elementary school years he became well known by the children as "Mr. Fisher," not as Levi, a second-class citizen with hayseeds in his hat. On rainy days he would pick me up from school in the "market wagon," permitting as many other children as could pack into the wagon to hop a ride home. I was proud when I looked out the school house window and saw that wagon coming slowly down the hill toward the school. That "Amish difference" enhanced, rather than detracted from, my popularity. If my father had related to outsiders awkwardly and apologetically, I would have felt something other than pride. My parents were socially comfortable and accepted themselves as different but equal.

Amish Patrolwoman

Because I was the only Amish child in my class in a large, consolidated town school, I did not have the opportunity to become part of an Amish clique. In school I became one of the group and totally identified with non-Amish students. I was a good student, the kind that made teachers feel worthwhile even when they had a tough teaching day. However, I was also very careful to maintain positive peer relationships so that I was not seen as "teacher's pet." I became a "patrolman" at the earliest age possible and in eighth grade was elected captain of a sizable patrol force, a status position. My parents were proud, I'm sure, of my achievements and the recognition I received for being a good student, but they did not reveal their pride. In their minds, school and formal education were not that important.

The availability of books and magazines in my home and my mother's keen curiosity and interest in world affairs were very instrumental in creating my thirst for more knowledge. Teachers became my role models and were powerful in reinforcing the quest to learn. My eighth-grade teacher played an advocacy role with my parents, convincing them to send me to ninth grade instead of making me repeat eighth grade until my fifteenth birthday, as was customary for Amish students. Several non-Amish professional friends such as the high school principal, the dentist's wife, and the town postmistress also played significant roles in kindling my educational fantasies.

Faltering Fantasies

The majority of Amish students looked forward to the time when they could "quit school" and become more totally involved in the life of the community. In contrast, I felt an overwhelming heaviness when I thought of dropping out of school. In good Amish style, I suppressed these heavy and anxious feelings. The summer following graduation from eighth grade, I had a "nervous breakdown." I experienced thoughts of suicide and overwhelming feelings of anxiety. I coped by withdrawing and refusing to get out of my bed and my room for a period of six to eight weeks.

During that summer, while working for my aunt who had fourteen children, I became vividly aware that I was leaving, or had left, Amish childhood, and that my fantasies about becoming a teacher or even a concert violinist were just that—fantasies. I had practiced a lot on my imaginary violin out behind the chicken house. Now childhood fantasies had to be put on the shelf. My childhood freedom was over; it was time to begin wearing a head covering and identifying myself as a young woman. I was being asked to put aside roller skating, bike and pony riding, playing hide-and-go-seek, and other games with town friends. The stark reality of my new role as hired girl was more than my emotional system could absorb. I loved my aunt and all of her fourteen children, but the reality of that future was very frightening.

Because of my breakdown, I started school later in the fall. That school year was a memorable one and I ended it feeling very isolated and alone. I began to rebel by resisting the pressures to conform to the Amish female role: cooking, sewing, and preparation of hope chest handiwork. Instead I began hiring myself out as a field hand, taking pride in my newly found identity of being able to "work as hard as a man." I had less and less contact with my non-Amish friends and began moving closer to my Amish peers.

I joined the Amish church with a very serious commitment at the age of sixteen. I did fantasize about adaptations, such as marrying someone who lived near a store and becoming a salesperson, or remaining single and becoming a veterinary assistant. At age twenty-one, at an Amish "singing" (young people's gathering), it seemed that an angel of the Lord appeared to me in the guise of a young Amish man from Indiana. He convinced me that I could go to college without a high school diploma.

In less than two months I had taken the necessary eligibility exams and had enrolled at a Mennonite college. Prior to enrollment, I told my Amish bishop about my desire to go to college so that I could become a good teacher. At that time there were several private, Amish schools in operation whose teachers had only an eighth-grade education. My bishop consulted with the larger bishop group and reluctantly gave his approval, saying that they preferred that I not go to college.

At college I was in the minority again with another group of non-Amish peers. I felt pressure periodically to conform, to be Mennonite. At times I felt somewhat confused theologically. Throughout my college years, I maintained the Amish garb and an overall positive attitude toward my Amish background. Since I was so entrenched in a culture which devalued higher education, the pursuit of education did not become an end in itself. It was a means to increased self-awareness, acquisition of teaching skills, and preparation for a mission to all those other Amish youth whom I assumed were thirsting for knowledge like I had.

Good-bye Amish

Between my junior and senior year, I was excommunicated from the Amish Church because of my professional pursuits. This was a very painful experience. I sought out my bishop several days before my excommunication, hoping to dissuade him. However, I think I needed some kind of emotional affirmation from him which I did receive. He was a just and a deeply caring person. I met him out in the field. I asked questions about education and sin and tried my best to make him understand that I wanted to continue both my education and my membership in the Amish community. He would not say that further education was sin and he agonized in his efforts to explain why excommunication was necessary if I would not repent. Both of us were sensitive and hurt deeply; we cried unashamedly.

After excommunication I began thinking of myself as a professional teacher. I joined the National Education Association. After the first year of teaching I began to accumulate credits by taking graduate courses. I was on my way to professionalism.

My first year of teaching was a good one. I worked with a

group of "low-achievers" who had serious images of being failures. The second year I had a "high-achiever" academic group. I was in a situation of "having arrived."

Some frustrations began building for me, though. I was coerced into working within a great "I AM" framework, passing judgment in the form of letter grades—a system in which a borderline student might never get a better grade than a D, even if he deserved an A for effort. After a second year of working with an academically gifted group, I yearned to move into a counseling role.

Hello Professionalism

Upon learning of the availability of a professional slot as school social worker, I decided to go in that direction. Undoubtedly, exposure to my Amish mother's nonprofessional, private "social work" practice contributed to my drive. My mother was pragmatic, supportive, confrontive, and highly skilled in her helping role as she "counseled" individuals in the Amish community. During my training at the University of Pennsylvania School of Social Work, I did need to learn how to accept differences. My mother had cultivated and modeled that skill far beyond its development in professional social work.

As I became involved in the professionalization process, I was often irritated by the intellectualization and the verbalization that was required of professional social workers. Simple, spontaneous human responses suddenly became complicated and were subjected to analysis and questioning. In one situation I was told my genuine tears of compassion were neither helpful nor professional.

I experienced a strong inner push toward professionalism, toward acquiring specific skills which would identify me as outstanding in the field of social work. With this pressure came an accompanying sense of anxiety that I wasn't making it to the top, that I might not be a super woman. Still, my formal professional process ended and I received my MSW degree. I had arrived. I had entered the helping profession. My colleagues and

I considered ourselves *helpers* and the "helpees" were our "clients" or "cases." I had been seduced to believe that I was now on another level, with a higher status than my clients. My sense of community and brotherhood became muddled as I tried to make accurate assessments and diagnoses of my client, in order to help him or her make necessary behavioral changes.

God in his infinite wisdom plopped me amidst a group of delinquent boys in Chicago for my first social work experience. These boys helped me by forcing me to take a look at myself and my newly acquired professional status, and by beginning to deprogram my professionalism.

And Back Again

I think my first conscious move away from professionalism was to stop using the possessive "my" when referring to the persons with whom I related. It seemed demeaning and dehumanizing for both of us when I referred to them as "my clients" or "my boys." In this deprogramming process, my old Amish values began to supersede my newly acquired professional value system. In professional jargon, I began translating the skills, values, and cultural framework that I had acquired as an Amish child into an "Amish or brotherhood" treatment modality.

For example, the Amish community holds a strong intrinsic value for human worth. There are many opportunities in the community to live out and demonstrate this value in everyday relationships. Assessments, diagnoses, and judgments are not important. Nor is there much of a focus on behavioral change, socialization, or even salvation. A person is worthy of being helped simply because he is part of the brotherhood or, if an outsider, simply because he is another human being who happens to need help. The act of helping is spontaneous caring, with few emotional "strings attached." When I began practicing social work within an Amish modality, I no longer saw clients categorically as delinquents. Their backgrounds and problems were less significant. These persons and their potential for brotherhood became more spontaneous and effective.

In examining my professional experiences over the past fifteen years, I've experienced a growing sense of success as I've been able to translate my Amish roots into my professional practice. My Amish values have been very powerful in enabling me to feel compassion and communicate caring. They have influenced many of my choices. For example, approximately ten years of my fifteen years in social work have been in residential settings, in small communities where the creation of a therapeutic milieu is primary. This type of setting gives me opportunity to be more Amish and less professional. It's considered therapeutic in these settings to go camping and jogging with "delinquent" boys or to become involved in gardening and furniture moving with "dependent" or "disturbed" young women with "poor self-images." In these settings it is acceptable to have lunch or dinner with one's "clients."

Over the years I've developed a therapeutic modality or way of relating which incorporates several Amish relational patterns such as confrontation, directness, and straightforwardness. Like my Amish bishop, I've been able to set limits for others with a great deal of caring and love so that the limits were not interpreted as rejection.

Throughout the past ten years I've been influenced by William Glasser's *Reality Therapy,* probably because of its primary emphasis on involvement. It also focuses on helping persons make responsible choices and plans for themselves, then committing themselves to that behavior. These are the techniques my mother used in her helping relationships in the Amish community.

Although I've made many adaptations in my process of becoming truly professional, the primary one has been translating the best of my Amish roots into my professional practice. Every Christian professional needs to identify and come to terms with his or her value system, and the need to relate to individuals in the context of fellowship community. We also need to identify our specific cultural roots and integrate these patterns into our professional relationships. Paradoxically, if we attempt to submerge these patterns from our backgrounds in our efforts to become professional, we will in fact become less professional.

Professionalism at its best can mean the use of our total self with its value system and cultural patterns within a relational context. As a Christian this means a person-to-person relationship, rather than a therapist-to-client, teacher-to-student, or doctor-to-patient relationship. Professionalism in a Christian context means servanthood, not a status of superiority over others.

CHAPTER FIVE

Psychiatric Technicians Emerge as a Political Power

By Ruth E. Krall

Conception

Individual professionals and their clients are not the sum total of professionalism. There is much more. A professional is identified with a particular community of professionals which has a life of its own. It may be a profession at the beginning of its life history or it may be a well-entrenched profession. In any case, professionals have more than clients to deal with: they also become entwined with the life, growth, perpetuation, and survival of the profession itself.

The life history of a profession begins long before it's ever identified as a profession. As groups of people actually perform the functions of a newly defined occupation, they develop skills and experience on the job. A pattern for doing this particular work begins to emerge. Persons who stay with the new occupation identify the core skills necessary for satisfactory performance. Soon skilled practitioners form technical schools to train others for entrance into the emerging profession. Sometimes the training occurs on the job. Teachers in these technical programs have frequently gained their expertise by work experience. They usually do not have formal academic preparation.

As the profession reaches its adolescence, a core of persons get advanced education and a subgroup of researchers and teachers emerges. A drive begins within the profession to have all training done within a college setting. Questions of educational accreditation soon emerge. Education and on-the-job training become required tickets for admittance of newcomers to the occupation.

A final step in the professionalizing process occurs when the occupation begins the internal struggle to separate the "true" professionals from the "less-than-professional" practitioners within the occupation's membership. The group studies its functions, codifies its standards, sets rigid entrance requirements, and decides who should be allowed to enter its educational programs. It then begins to delegate some of its "dirty work" to persons it calls nonprofessionals or paraprofessionals.

Gestation: 1945-1952

I will examine the professionalizing process in the life history of psychiatric technicians within the state of California from 1945 to 1969. In California, as in the rest of the nation in the mid-1940s, the state hospital system was the major institution designed to care for the mentally ill. California had twelve separate state institutions with a combined capacity for 40,000 patients. These hospitals were staffed predominantly by psychiatric attendants. In 1948 only 45 registered nursing positions were actually filled in the state system. All other positions were filled with psychiatric attendants. Their educational preparation was 45 hours of structured, on-the-job training.

California at this time followed the national practice of recruiting whoever would work with the mentally ill and of paying them as little as possible. While many of these psychiatric attendants were humane, some of them were as disturbed as the patients for whom they cared. Alcoholism, sadistic or sociopathic behaviors, and sexual deviations were not unusual among certain groups of psychiatric attendants. Some of the attendants were functionally illiterate. In one state hospital, I watched an attendant pour and administer medications. He could not read nor write. He only knew where to make a check mark and sign his initial.

In 1950 the California Department of Mental Hygiene developed a mandatory, statewide curriculum for all of its attendants. The attendants were renamed "psychiatric technicians." As a part of upgrading the occupational image, the technicians organized themselves; in 1950 the California Society of Psychiatric Technicians (CSPT) was founded with two goals: (a) to upgrade the quality of psychiatric services to the mentally ill and (b) to improve the economic base of state-employed, psychiatric technicians.

Birth: 1952-1955

In 1952 the California Society of Psychiatric Technicians (CSPT) raised the issue of licensure and the creation of a separate licensing board to regulate the practice of psychiatric technology. A California Senate Interim Committee on Nurse Problems heard testimony on this proposal. The committee introduced a Senate bill to initiate discussion on this issue. The State Department of Mental Hygiene supported mandatory licensure and the separate, regulatory board. However, the powerful California Hospital Association opposed the bill on the basis of predicted increased costs to private agencies. The California Nurses' Association fought the bill, arguing that a psychiatric technician's work lay in the province of nursing. No legislative action was taken and the bill died in committee.

Childhood: 1955-1957

In 1955, the CSPT introduced a permissive licensure bill. Hearings were again held. Opposition testimony by the California Hospital Association focused on the threat of increased costs to private hospitals. As in 1952, the California Nurses' Association tried to kill the licensure bill by arguing that psychiatric technology was a part of the nursing role and function. As such, it was covered by the nursing regulatory agency of the state.

The Senate Interim Committee on Licensing Business and Professions, in its concluding report to the Senate, noted that one of the key objectives of the psychiatric technicians was to establish additional dignity and prestige for their profession.

The Senate Business and Professions Committee said that licensure was not necessary to protect the public since the psychiatric technicians already had to pass civil service examinations to work in state agencies. The committee concluded that:

> One of the principle reasons of such licensing laws as is proposed would be to establish dignity for the profession and to create a status for those engaged in it. These are not the objectives of a licensing program.... Civil Service status serves the function of creating dignity and security for state employees. (California Senate: 1957a)

Adolescence: 1957-1965

In 1957 State Senator Alan Short was chairman of a powerful committee, the Senate Interim Committee on the Treatment of Mental Illness. This committee was responsible for a revolution of California's mental health delivery system. One part of its work was to hear the continuing debate on the psychiatric technician licensure issue. Senator Short's firm commitment to the mentally ill of California was a potent force that helped the technicians to move toward their goal of licensure.

This time the California Nurses' Association led the opposition by again arguing that in-service training alone was not adequate to qualify a psychiatric technician for a license. CSPT and the California State Employees Association both gave pro-licensure testimony. The Department of Mental Hygiene testified for the licensure program. On the one side were the CSPT, the California State Employee's Association, the State Department of Mental Hygiene, and the Senate subcommittee, all of whom were advocating technician licensure. On the other side were the California Hospital Association, the California Nurses' Association, and the California Medical Association.

The powerful alliance of the Department of Mental Hygiene with the Senate Subcommittee on Psychiatric Technicians forced the allied health organizations to cooperate with each other in defining an acceptable and politically viable licensure bill. The professions and their lobbying organizations met and established a compromise bill which was introduced into the Senate. With the powerful endorsement from all the health organizations, and with the subsequent removal of all formal opposition, the California legislature provided a permissive certification act for California's psychiatric technicians. The title, Certified Psychiatric Technician, was limited to those technicians who met the requirements of the statute.

Adulthood: 1965-1969

By 1968 California was phasing out its large state hospital system in favor of a local, decentralized system of care. Community mental health centers, county governments, and private agencies were providing most of the mental health services within the state. These decentralized facilities were not required to use the state educated and certified persons. While the state system had an established salary range of $15,000-18,000, the decentralized, local agencies frequently utilized untrained, uncertified psychiatric aides. Agencies could and did pay these persons salaries at or below $10,000. While these aides could not claim to be Certified Psychiatric Technicians, they performed the same types of personal and therapeutic services.

Certified technicians began to realize their occupational vulnerability. With an eroding state hospital base for employment, 10,000 to 12,000 persons could soon be unemployed in an occupation for which they had trained and in which they were certified.

One of the real issues behind the rhetoric of patient welfare was that of economic security and survival. A mandatory licensure bill would force private agencies to hire only Certified Psychiatric Technicians to do psychiatric technology. Technicians were concerned that they have work throughout the state as the state moved to decentralized, local programs for treatment of the mentally ill. Requiring mandatory certification or licensure meant that certified technicians could remain employed. In addition, licensure would likely mean maintaining state level salaries in every psychiatric setting, public or private.

Technicians were concerned that they not be replaced in California's mental health system with either untrained psychiatric aides or with registered nurses.

From 1960 on, two psychiatric technician lobbying groups intensively lobbied the California Senate, House, and governor. By 1965, technicians were requesting a mandatory licensure act. Mandatory licensure would prohibit untrained and unlicensed persons from practicing psychiatric technology in California. In addition, it would provide economic security for technicians trained in state hospitals. Education began to be seen as one route to obtaining such a licensure act. Specific curriculums were developed within California's vast junior college system.

In each legislative session from 1965 to 1969, the major lobbying associations were alive and active. Predictably, the California Nurses' Association argued that psychiatric technician functions were a part of nursing. The California Hospital Association reactivated its earlier stance of concern for cost control for private, psychiatric hospitals. The California Medical Association insisted on maintaining and protecting the issue of medical control of all psychiatric services performed in the state. Their lobbying effort was primarily directed toward the inclusion of the phrase, "who under the direction of a licensed physician, performs services for. . . ."

The psychiatric technician lobbying groups in Sacramento demanded the following:

- full autonomy from control by registered nurses and licensed physicians
- education within the state's junior college system
- salaries in the private sector that equalled those in the state hospital system
- mandatory licensure to control entry into and practice within the occupation
- prohibition of practice by non-licensed psychiatric aides
- creation of a separate state regulatory board

Finally, in 1969 the psychiatric technicians capitulated on some of their demands. A bill was submitted which included medical and nursing control and which maintained technician licensing within the nursing regulatory board. In exchange, the technicians got support from all the allied health groups for legislation which gave them:

- an education base within the junior college system
- mandatory licensure with provisions which controlled entrance into psychiatric technician educational programs and into work settings
- a negotiating basis for a salary range in the private sector that was roughly equivalent to the salary structure in the state system

In summary, over a twenty-five-year period the professionalizing process for California's licensed psychiatric technicians involved:

- a name change from psychiatric attendant to licensed psychiatric technician
- setting minimal educational requirements of at least one year at the junior college level
- requiring successful performance on a licensing examination
- successful negotiations with the allied health professions
- gaining control of entrance requirements
- gaining partial control over rules and regulations
- creating economic dependency in patient care settings since mental health agencies could no longer employ unskilled and uneducated psychiatric aides
- creating a powerful, ongoing lobbying effort toward independent and autonomous practice

Shabby Compassion

The lobbying process to achieve mandatory licensure involved the conflict of vested interests within the public and private sectors of the mental health community in California. Many of these interests were tied to economics. Ideals of service to the mentally ill were subsumed in the economic battles. Patient welfare was a sacred cow which each side used as the basis for its testimony in legislative hearings. One significant motivator for psychiatric technicians was that of economic and professional survival in a time when California was changing its patterns of providing services to the mentally ill.

During this time of rapid change in the state hospital system, the role and function of the state-educated and permissively certified psychiatric technician was threatened in a free market. California technicians skillfully utilized the powers of the state to create an ongoing, albeit somewhat artificial, demand for licensed psychiatric technicians. Powers of the state were established to enforce provisions of the licensure act. All of this occurred even though there is no demonstrable, empirical evidence that licensure improves the quality of care available to the mentally ill. The process used by technicians in California is at work throughout the United States in a variety of disciplines and professions.

As a Christian professional, I am ambivalent about professionalization. I believe that health care technology and specialization mandate some guarantee of safe practice for the lay public. Personal, mandatory licensure is the mechanism by which the state can best regulate safe practice. At the same time I know that mandatory licensure has the side effect of creating an elitist, powerful group that controls the public's access to services and that contributes to the growing inability to control health care costs within this country.

Within all of the health professions, I have seen issues of power, status, economics, and interdisciplinary control shabbily dressed in the language of "compassion for clients and their welfare." I have seen high costs for inept and inadequate care. I have seen agencies torn apart by interdisciplinary conflicts and battles for control and power.

As I reflect upon the power struggles and conflicts which I have seen and experienced, I have an increasing disquietude about professionalization. I am firmly committed to competency of practice within the professions. But I doubt that we can control the pressures toward elitism. I wonder about the possibility of relating across discipline boundaries in ways which reveal that we are sisters and brothers to one another. I ponder the questions, "How do we remain servants of each other and of all our fellow humans? How do we have compassion for those who need our services? How do we maintain safe standards for all care given?"

I am greatly distressed by the antagonistic professional relationships that exist within the health care system. Church agencies, as well as secular ones, are torn by internal power struggles. Physicians and nurses, psychologists and physicians, nurses and psychiatric technicians, psychologists and social workers fight with each other and with agency administrators for status, control, and protection of professional turf. Professional antagonisms frequently become personal vendettas, a clash of raw power.

In the community of faith we must begin to search for new models of providing human services. We need to open our professionalized selves to our brothers and sisters for their critique and advice. We must voluntarily give up the power that is associated with being a "true professional." We must ask for insight into and healing of our divisions and of our divisiveness. We must actively practice peacemaking and conflict resolution. While I do not see a clear way out of the morass that results from our professionalism, I know that we must begin the search together.

The Impact of Professionalism

CHAPTER SIX

The Impact of Professionalism on Persons

By David W. Augsburger

Professionalism and Personhood?

A PhD—is it an abbreviation for personhood? Or a new improved, larger-than-life edition of the same? Or perhaps a replacement for personhood. Maybe a PhD should come with these instructions: "Open trap door X (See figure A); remove outmoded personhood. Insert new professionalism. Be certain all contact points are firmly in place so entire unit is activated by new core element. Discard old self in safe, permanent disposal."

The above fantasy first flashed for me when doing therapy with a young couple in deep trouble on the eve of his graduation. (I, too, was nearing completion of a doctorate so the transference was instant and open.)

"Frankly," he told her, "you don't fit anymore. We've nothing in common, you've nothing in common with my friends, you don't want any of my lifestyle as a professional; there's just no place for you in my life." All this was said, not in anger, but in sad recognition that they had grown far apart.

"I don't know you anymore. Once you spoke with me as one human being to another. Now you're not there. I speak to you and a stranger answers."

She, in financing his education had become, as he said, "incurably blue collar." He, living off her generosity, had become, in her words, "a professional prig."

An outdated personhood, uncared for during the rigors of

"higher education," can be discarded as one opts for the attractions of the appropriate professionalism. Or personhood can be updated, integrated, matured in the process of achieving professional skills and standing. Recognizing the high demands of becoming a professional, it is no surprise that something less pressing will need to be sacrificed. There goes the time required to keep selfhood growing at the same pace as scholastic growth.

Physician, Professor, Pastor, Person

A physician speaks: "The schedule, the demands, the financial obligations in establishing a new practice, the overload necessary to work myself to a position where I could invite another doctor to join me—if it was any of these, it was all of these that turned me into a twenty-four-hour-a-day, seven-days-a-week workaholic. I'd joked about others I had known who had no sense of their limitations, then I did the same thing." Four years into the practice of medicine, and Dr. Miller is discovering that his personhood is totally eclipsed by the "professional identity" he accepted with the degree, the license, the office, and the stethoscope.

A professor speaks: "You're feeling frustrated that you rang up the wrong price and you're wanting me to buy a pack of Rolaids to make it come out even?" The speaker paying for lunch is Dr. Allen, a psychologist who talks counselorese and exudes empathy even to her Datsun. "You're missing on one cylinder and feeling a need for tune-up?" The ability to just be Joan Allen disappeared during one of her internships. She hasn't missed it yet. Assuming a full-time professional identity eliminated so many little interpersonal conflicts and routine tensions by allowing her to relate to people from the safe distance of a smooth, helping style. The fact that she is less personal is well hidden by her proficiency in "being facilitative."

A pastor speaks: "Now that you are pastors, there are four traits that will be expected of you. Father figure that you are, you will be like your Father in heaven: omniscient, with words for every occasion; omnipotent, with the promise of strength for every problem; omnipresent, because you're expected to be everywhere at once; and immutable, always a pastor, always pastoral."

The speaker is a pastor to pastors, lecturing young ministers on the nature of pastoral identity. For him, becoming a pastor is like being a total woman, an all-consuming passion. The whole self is invested, the profession defines one's identity. Personhood is swallowed up, digested, assimilated, and supplies the cellular tissue for the new professionalism.

"The trouble with putting the collar on," Ugandan churchman Festo Kivengere once told a group of ministers, "is that it will not stay a one-inch band of white; it grows on you. No sooner is it in place than it grows up the neck and elevates the chin. You can see the young minister walking around, chin in the air, with inflated self-esteem. Then it covers the jaw and he loses all personal determination, decisiveness, and will. Then it masks the mouth and you can't understand a thing he says. Soon it seals in the nose, and he loses all sense of discrimination and discernment. It creeps over the eyes and he can see nothing but the collar. Once over the forehead, and independent thought is gone. All too soon, there's nothing but collar. He looks like a filter tip. All is filtered through the collar."

All too quickly, too easily, too seductively the struggle to mature as persons is yielded over to the drive to succeed as professionals. The impact of professionalism on personal identity is visible not only to counselors and therapists, but to spouses, children, and friends. It is the person experiencing this change who often fails to be self-reflective, since he or she is caught up in establishing the self in productivity. Viewing this professional-personal dilemma as a natural, normal, and neutral rite of passage in life, rather than a hazard to be avoided, may help us to see it in the perspective of the normal developmental journey.

Infancy, Industry, Identity, Intimacy, Productivity, Integrity

The helpful maps to human maturation through the middle years, charted for us by Erik Erikson, offer insight into the sequence of tasks a person completes throughout the seasons of life.

Infancy: Upon the childhood basis of trust and hope (the first year), is built autonomous self-direction and will (the second and third years). To this is added initiative and purpose (the dramatic playful experimentation with roles from ages three to six).

Industry: Now in the school years—six to twelve—the child is set to the tasks of learning industry, of achieving competence and demonstrating the perfection of performance skills. Overcoming feelings of inferiority and incompetence prepare the person for working at identity.

Identity: Youth is the time of identity formation. If one is dogged by unfinished crises from the past—an overburden of mistrust, shame, doubt, guilt, and/or inferiority—achieving an identity may be a particularly painful process. It can be frozen or postponed, or solved by accepting a foreign or familiar identity second hand.

Intimacy: By the end of the second decade of life, identity reaches out for intimacy, the I seeks a Thou. The intimacy work of the late teens and early twenties finds its fulfillment as the person learns to love.

Productivity: Life tasks become foreground, and the ability to generate work, to care about one's contribution to present and future generations, to take one's place within the productive community become a central task of the three middle decades of life.

The pressures of graduate training can mobilize so many of the old drives to prove competence that a person can regress to the emotional state of adolescence (achieving renewed industry and competence by overcoming a sense of inferiority) and emerge with an identity centered in one's new acquisition of professional skills, abilities, and status. (Back to industry to finish those leftover feelings of inferiority! Get it right this time. Now I've got another degree to certify my competence. This is who I am, my new professional self. At last an identity that is safe. Secure. Salable. There, now I know *who* I am—a doctor, a professor, a nurse, a pastor—or is that *what* I am?")

Achieving productivity as the reward of one's industry can so easily be taken as a confirmation that professional identity has been earned and, along with it, the right to make it one's whole identity.

Integrity: The goal of maturation is not identity, although I must know who I am to mature or the self that matures may be only a maturing copy of someone less mature. The goal is integrity, and integrity is not achieved; rather, integrity is identity grown wise through the integration of all of life—identity, intimacy, and productivity into a unified whole. Who I am, whose I am, what I do or am combine to fulfill an integrated sense of mature wisdom. Any marriage of identity and productivity impoverishes both. An identity which accepts a profession's boundaries for its own has too willingly sacrificed its possibilities for personhood. A productivity which usurps a person's identity silences the "I" which can move freely to correct, direct, and create the personal maturation process.

Person, Profession

The professionalism which we need is an expression of authentic personhood.

The experience of personhood advocated here is a particularly Western and peculiarly Christian view of personality. It is not to be confused with the contrasting Western tradition of "individualism" which is a view of the self as competitive, disconnected from others, acquisitive, mercenary, and ultimately egotistical. Personhood, as an opposite conception of selfhood, is noncompetitive, integrative, communitarian; it values self and others as equal parts of the wholeness of humanness.

Individualism may well be the vice our world is suffering under more deeply than any other. In personhood lie the possibilities of wholeness, healing, and human health.

The professionalism which frees both the one who serves and the one served emerges from the depths of genuine personhood experienced and expressed as the exercise of personal power within and for community.

The professional who expresses full personhood is identified by six characteristics, occurring as a cluster of traits.

First, the professional is a learned and learning person. As an educated person, he or she has mastered and is continually mastering some body of knowledge. This is wise personhood.

Second, the professional is a skilled and skillful person. As a practicing expert in some specific cluster of skills, he or she has the requisite talents, necessary learnings, and the crucial sharpening by practice under supervision. He or she applies these skills to life situations. This is skilled personhood.

Third, the professional is an institutional and communal person. As a participant in a particular community of fellow professionals and a part of a social institution serving that community, he or she becomes a servant to a historical, local, actual human community. This is communal personhood.

Fourth, the professional is an accountable and responsible person. As a practitioner, he or she acts responsibly according to clear standards of competence, ethics, and interpersonal respect which are in relationships of continuing accountability to peers and to society. This is responsible personhood.

Fifth, the professional is an integrated and centered person. As a thinker, feeler, actor, he or she has achieved a significant level of congruence to act, work with integrity, and to respond with centered intentions. This is integrated personhood.

Sixth, the professional is a committed and value-oriented person. As one dedicated to service, he or she is clearly concerned for others as well as for self; social welfare and personal well-being are equally important. As a value-oriented person, the principles of equal love, shared power, and mutual justice shape his or her service to humankind. This is committed personhood.

Such professionalism is an extension of and an expression of a shared experience of personhood-in-community. Such a person is at heart an eternal amateur, while in action a practicing professional.

The Amateur Professional

It is instructive to note that the word "amateur" is not to be used in opposition to the term "professional," but as a central sustaining core. Amateur comes from the Latin "amator," meaning "lover," one who does something because he or she loves to do it. He who serves for the joy of it or for love of it does that service or that action from the heart. The chronic suspicion of "the cold professional," in contrast, visualizes a person who is efficient in function but empty of the requisite human caring, with a passion for performance but little compassion for service.

The "amateur" continues to be "amator" who is forever "amorous" in the act of loving service. The person-valuing core of the amateur-professional sustains the caring motivation, the concerned self-giving, the compassionate sharing of person-to-person.

I am I.
I see, I think, I feel, I will, I act.
I am who I am, I am what I am.

I have learned.
I receive, I reflect, I value, I integrate, I express.
I am one who is learned, I am one learning.

I can do.
I observe, I respond, I care, I intervene, I serve.
I am skilled. I am more than my skills.

I am. I have learned.
I can do all this
Within the community of Christ
Which strengthens me. (Phil. 4:11-14.)

Why I'm a Volunteer Professional

By Elaine Stoltzfus

"I'm Elaine Stoltzfus and I'm a teacher." (Pause) "Part time." (Pause) "I work as a volunteer."

We were introducing ourselves around the circle at a weekend seminar. The exercise was the usual "what is your name and what do you do" formality that identifies you either as someone with a profession or the spouse of a professional.

The typical mental pictures follow: "teacher" evokes an image of a professional, albeit on the bottom rung; "part time" casts a shadow on that image. Such a person must not be completely serious or committed. Perhaps she just wants to get out of the house. But it's the word "volunteer" that clouds everything. Aha! She couldn't get a regular position; probably she lacks the proper qualifications; she means she's an aide, not a teacher.

But I **am** a teacher, certified in both New York and Pennsylvania. I have eight years teaching experience in public schools, and am six credits shy of a master's degree in education. And I've been offered a "real" job in our public school.

My decision to work as a volunteer reading teacher at the local sheltered workshop developed as I tried to put together my commitment to use a God-given teaching gift with the fact that our family does not need an additional income to meet our needs. The sheltered workshop has no money to pay a remedial reading teacher, yet the clients there often lack the reading skills needed to get a job.

So with the affirmation of my church community, as well as its agreement to pay for my reading materials, I have been practicing my profession without pay for the past three-and-one-half years. Sometimes I wonder what that says to the people around me in my Appalachian setting. She's rich enough to be a volunteer? She can indulge her whims to do something different, with the option to withdraw whenever she tires of the novelty? That's not what I want to communicate, however.

I want my work to witness to the fact that I care about people, that I am called by God to use my talent for others. Being a volunteer teacher and a Christian brings with it special responsibilities. My style of living must be consistent with my motives for being a volunteer. And my attitude on the job needs to be serious in terms of punctuality, attendance, and lesson planning. That's not always easy. When my children need to stay home from school because of illness, I stay home too, rather than getting a baby-sitter. Would I do that if I had a paid position? I continually need to evaluate my motives and work style to make sure I am giving my best, "as unto the Lord."

I believe God uses the body of believers to direct us, whether as volunteers or as earning professionals, in using our gifts. I need the continued affirmation and support of the church. This frees me from having to be defensive about my work status with those who question it. The work I do makes sense to me because I am part of a church that takes me seriously as a volunteer professional.

CHAPTER SEVEN

The Impact of Professionalism on Marriages

By Phyllis Pellman Good

When I was seventeen I figured that my love of English ruled out my loving a man. Not that I believed I didn't have the capacity for both! But where in my world was the young woman with a successful marriage and career? So as a hedge against disappointment, and with an appetite for literature, I set out to study to teach the classics.

It was a conscious choice I made. Marriage, I thought, did not have room for two professionals. Since my imagination couldn't cough up a convincing figure of me as Married Woman, I settled for what seemed the more likely future me, Professional Woman.

In the years since my private little battle, the apparent choices are no longer so clearly cut or limited. Married professional people are part of our families, neighborhoods, and congregations. They come in different combinations: One, a husband who is an active professional and a wife who is a nonprofessional (there are lots of these); two, a husband who is an active professional and a wife who is a nonpracticing professional, for a variety of interesting reasons (this combination is also abundant); three, a husband who is an active professional and a wife who is an active professional (a comparatively rare situation); four, a husband who is a nonprofessional and a wife who is an active professional (highly unusual).

The options have increased. But rare is the couple where each is fulfilled professionally, and whose marriage is flourishing. But before we romanticize history, were marriages really better when neither husband nor wife were college-educated professionals and both struggled to keep the farm and the herd producing and seven (give or take a few) little souls thriving?

The business of cultivating a happy marriage partnership has always required immense tending, fierce commitment, and a mix of good humor and vulnerability. Despite our education and sophisticated psychology, successful marriages still have the same basic requirements. What *has* changed is our sociology and self-understanding. Those switches have implications for marriages.

A Few Facts

Women no longer spend most of their adult lives rearing children. Families are smaller; less energy is needed to feed, clothe, and shelter youngsters than before. So there are more women in the labor force than ever. (A 1980 issue of *Money* claims that 57 percent of all women between the ages of 20 and 64 work outside the home.) Because a career is now possible, many women are choosing occupations and training for them. Consequently, professional women are fast becoming the norm rather than the exception.

Many professional men and many professional women choose to marry. Those with careers often postpone marriage; there seems to be no movement among these groups to reject marriage, however. The odds look promising: people wait to marry until they are more mature, financially stable, and certain of their own identity. But if marriages operate on the ideal of "I love you as much as I love me," the professional who has little training in self-sacrifice and putting the other person first, may have a tough adjustment.

Be it a marriage of two practicing professionals or one active professional and one not, tensions may center on this point: although schooled to believe I am an expert (with all the attendant perks), that attitude and behavior must be put away at home. Marriage requires the antithesis of professional power codes—not insisting on management or the final word, not relegating "menial" jobs—in short, not exercising power over another.

So while the odds are great that a professional who is about to marry brings more maturity age-wise, greater financial stability and satisfaction about his or her job to the altar than the nonprofessional, there are some other hazards to be aware of. One is not necessarily more enlightened in personal life because one holds an advanced degree or membership in a professional organization.

The Gap

Marriage, at its best, is a partnership with two people sharing responsibilities and equality in decision making. Ideally one's professional status should have no bearing on one's marriage relationship. But a combination of forces can play havoc with those intentions.

Traditional roles and expectations have formidable strength. "Should I or should I not be working?" goes along with lots of women to their offices. The same question haunts scores of women who choose to stay home. ("Why do people act like I can't think anymore?" asked my friend who had just had her first baby and had resigned her job to take care of him.) A recent study of men in college revealed that many assume that the man is the breadwinner; that although his wife may have a career, it is secondarily important to his own; and that the wife will stay home with preschool children. So while it seems to be true that husbands experience greater marital satisfaction if their wives are fulfilled in their day-to-day lives; there is a lot of uncertainty about the extent to which women, especially, should pursue careers. Men, on the other hand, are under pressures to be faithful to wife, family, and profession—all in proper proportion. So blame bounces around; guilt abounds. And for a people whose history and tradition value family highly, balancing career and home demands is especially tricky.

First the Hazards

There are hazards in every marriage where one or both partners is a professional. That is not to imply that one can marry free of risks, or that professionals should not marry. Professions make intensive demands on time, expect resolute loyalty; they often require travel and overwork, and produce stress and pressure. They also create fulfillment and satisfaction for their members. So without careful attention, a highly demanding profession is likely to be at war with the powerful claims of a marriage. (Children simply redeem or aggravate the situation.) But it is questionable whether the union of one or two professionals is on any more treacherous footing than a marriage of nonprofessionals where one or both spouses are preoccupied with physical and economic survival. Nor is it safe to assume that if an active professional marries a nonprofessional or someone who is willing to lay aside his or her career, that a deadlock is broken. "I'd leave him if I didn't love him," one doctor's wife burst out. Committed to her husband and children, she had put aside her nursing career and was now struggling to cope with his 75-hour work weeks. Each situation has the potential for satisfaction or disaster.

A marriage where one of the partners is a professional is likely to be more financially secure than one where neither is a professional. If both spouses are professionals, financial security increases nearly proportionately.

In fact, a woman's income may allow her husband to look for a more fulfilling job, go back to school, turn down a transfer, get rid of overtime; in short, it can reduce anxiety and overwork.

Two incomes also provide the opportunity for more independence. Despite that, few marriages of professionals break up for financial reasons. Many marriages of nonprofessionals, however, falter because of money stress.

Job satisfaction spills over at home. People content in their careers come home content. Beyond that, definitive statistics are fuzzy. It appears that women who work by choice in jobs for which they are trained, on a part-time schedule, are happier than those who work of necessity. Some men experience more marital satisfaction and less tension when their wives are happily employed; others face greater pressure and lower marital fulfillment than the husbands whose wives are at home full time. The reasons are multiple and complex.

There is a menacing gap between behavior and attitudes. Many husbands have been prepared to be the breadwinner, but with the promise of a backup at home. Their wives may have planned to be homemakers, never expecting the loneliness and feelings of desertion that go with marrying a busy professional. Other women feel enriched by going out to work; their husbands may feel deflated about picking up housework. And so, with the fulfillment experienced by many husbands and wives in their individual careers comes a heavy dose of role confusion tension.

A working woman may find success, self-confidence, and prestige by being good at her profession rather than from being an excellent homemaker. That may enhance or undermine a marriage. Money is seldom a worry, but who makes supper and does the wash is. Housework, calculated at requiring anywhere from 20 to 60 hours a week, gets less attention in households where husband and wife both work outside the home. By dropping standards and increasing efficiency, time for housework can often be sliced in half. Yet, caught between an old and new world, husbands may chafe about household neglect or being expected to help; women may shoulder the housework and, with it, anger about adding that to other work.

If one professional in a household can cause a hectic family schedule, two professionals can double the dilemma. Finding time alone together for family and for church becomes a herculean task. (It may be wise to treat your night-a-week for the family as a professional meeting; nothing may bump it from the schedule.) Meshing vacation times consumes energy. So does trying to keep one's partner abreast of one's own professional activities. The threat of a widening distance between husband and wife is always there. It is no less there when one spouse is an active professional and the other is not. Dividing up worlds and making independent decisions may begin to happen necessarily. But it is a trend that needs watching.

There are more sticky questions when one or both of a couple are professionals:

- •Where shall we locate—near his best job prospect or hers?
- •What happens to me and my self-respect if your career takes off and you suddenly become successful (especially if I worked to put you through school)?
- •Will we, after investing heavily in careers, have enough energy left for each other and our life together?
- •Should we have children and, if so, who will care for them?

No answers come easily. The matter of children is perhaps the most difficult. For although working women tend to have fewer children, it seems we are not entering an era of childlessness. People continue to want children. So for those professionals who plan a family, settling the question of who assumes their primary care may require considerable flexibility—from one or both parents. Housework can be neglected; child care cannot be.

Many women who continue their careers after becoming mothers go to work a little less primly than before, struggling with guilt and feeling the need to be a superwoman. "All I do is juggle my job, children, home, housework, and husband. What do I get? Guilt and sheer exhaustion, physically and emotionally," says one worn-out working mama. At this point the partnership in many marriages goes on the skids. Daddy may diaper, but when he leaves for work in the morning, he goes freer of anxiety about his child than mommy does.

Who is responsible for making a home, finally? Can or should one spouse take primary responsibility for the marriage and family while the other shoulders a career? To what extent is the concept of partnership possible?

What to Do

This is not a time for giving up either marriages or professions. Both are with us, in one shape or another, and will be for a long time. This is instead a time for marrying with the utmost care. Falling in love had better be surrounded with alertness and deliberation. Professionals who are married need all the maturity they can muster. Without it they may keep their career, but they won't keep their spouse.

Unfortunately, there are few models of successful marriages where both spouses have found partnership *and* fulfillment in their careers (whether at home or in a profession). It's a stiff climb, and one that doesn't end. In addition to love, two people need to bring some less romantic qualities to their marriage: respect for each other (no matter what either's professional status is); willingness to be vulnerable (not considered a virtue in professional circles); the commitment to spend time together at the risk of needing to say "no" to the voracious appetite of one's profession and its demand for time (like the Mennonite pastor who refused to meet a visiting Mennonite leader on his only evening in the area because it conflicted with the pastor's family night); the deliberate attempt to collaborate rather than compete, no matter the size of the issue at hand ("My time is more valuable than yours" is an assumption strictly out of bounds).

There are attitudes to cultivate. Perhaps the hardest and yet most basic is servanthood. It must be learned and kept in shape, the same as one's profession. If that ideal prevails in one's mind and behavior, the dominant grip of one's profession is weakened. That may create plusses at home and fallout at work. And since home and office are connected by a person, the balance inside him or her doesn't happen without tensions. "I feel defeated no matter what I do" becomes an often repeated chorus.

A community of faith can help sort issues, find solutions, give support. But here too is a catch: the more vital such a group becomes to its members, the more time and energy it requires. The professional who wants discipline and help must deliberately make room for it. It is also a major psychological step for him or her away from the individualism of the professional world.

The church community itself needs a bottomless supply of honesty, patience, forgiveness, and love if it intends to shelter marriages involving professionals. There is energy required of everyone on this issue—husband, wife, and the community with which they ally.

A couple can set up practices to nourish their relationships and to keep their professions partly at bay. They may decide to take no (or a limited amount of) work home, to save evenings and weekends for family, to vacation together, to be active in a local church. Household tasks can be delegated, thus taking the burden off the wife, removing the irritation of not having certain jobs done, and showing that no one in the household is above doing chores.

Husband and wife may both choose to work part time, especially after children join the family. That may result in a detriment to careers, yet if both spouses do it, there is more equality. There will likely also be fewer dollars than if one of the partners maintains a full-time job.

One can lobby for flexible work hours. This is not the way to go to the head of your profession, but it is one way to stay closer to your family. Flexible work hours do not fit with all jobs. When they do, employees may choose their own starting and quitting times; often they must work during certain "core" hours, and put in a specified number of hours per week.

There is a movement to enact fairer Social Security laws that would recognize the homemaker's contribution in a family where she is not a wage earner. Such a move, if enacted, could bolster the self-respect and raise the regard of others for the wife who chooses to stay home.

If one lives by default, one's marriage will dwindle to formalities and one's soul will be with one's profession. Only with a common conviction, purpose, and mind, and with constant care, can two people stay married to each other instead of their careers. A commitment made once is not enough. The specifics of that trust will be always shifting, brought about by promotions, setbacks, children. It behooves professionals who marry to be well armed with imagination, resourcefulness, cooperation, and a mind to put the other person first if they want a marriage and career that both work.

CHAPTER EIGHT

The Impact of Professionalism on Families

By Carl Rutt

Dear Dad,
   Lots of people have told me you are a great man. I believe that. I remember seeing your name in our local paper a lot when I was growing up. You were either president of a medical group or in charge of a special fact-finding committee or the speaker at a conference of physicians. I knew you were important. Your countless recognitions were proof of that. And you never forgot a birthday. I remember I always received an airmail special delivery letter from somewhere back East. But how I longed for you to be home and share my day with me. You were up so early and came home when we were all in bed.
   Yes, you've given me a lot, dad, and I appreciate it. I'm educated, I'm well traveled, I know about music and art, but I wish you'd had the time to really know me, because all I have are the newspaper clippings and the awards and the pictures. I don't really know you at all.

Your loving daughter

These poignant excerpts from a letter by a physician's daughter illustrate in stereotypical fashion potential problems when a parent is a professional (*Physician's Daughter,* 1975).

Professional Stereotypes

   The changes the family is experiencing as an institution in our culture today—smaller families, the breakdown in family life resulting from divorce, decreased ties with the extended family, and increased mobility—are so well known they need no elaboration. These changes have multiple causes; frequently these factors are found in professional families, although perhaps for different reasons than in nonprofessional families. For example, mobility often results from a positive choice between several attractive job opportunities, rather than it being forced on the family because the wage earner has been laid off. In addition, smaller families allow the career-oriented wife to begin her professional life sooner.

Every professional's family encounters positive or negative stereotypes; being "special" affects each family member. There is the "preacher's kid" who *should* be well behaved, but isn't; he brings discredit to his family, especially to his father. Teachers' children are expected to be properly studious, physicians' children to stay in perfect health, and dentists' children to have pearly white teeth. Such unrealistic expectations to be model children place undue pressure on the professionals' children. Too much pressure to conform to cultural expectations backfires eventually. Children and adolescents are ingenious at embarrassing parents at their points of greatest sensitivity. "What will my church think of me," the pastor wonders, "if they see Johnny having his tantrums?"

A friend remarked some years ago that in her former city, home of a huge medical clinic, children of physicians were quickly pigeonholed as "doctors' children." I was being recruited for a job by the clinic there, and this was one of several factors which led us to look elsewhere.

After arriving in our current location, we enrolled our daughter, Lesley, in a respected private school for kindergarten and first grade. The school was noted for its small class sizes and emphasis on self-paced learning. However, the high percentage of doctors' and lawyers' families there troubled us. We eventually transferred her to a city school where she could still learn at her own pace. We don't want our children to develop class prejudices or to feel elitist; we want them to accept others for what they are.

Professional parents need to be alert to both positive and negative prejudices and the impact they may have on family life. Occasionally the family members may be awarded extra privileges because of their prestigious social position. Perhaps a child's problem in school may not be dealt with in a routine manner, out of reluctance to confront the family promptly. Also, some professionals, because of feeling "special," avoid dealing with internal family problems out of embarrassment, guilt, or denial.

Many professions provide families with upper-middle-class financial status, although great wealth usually comes from business success (or the good fortune of surviving a "rich uncle"). The wise stewardship of money is a constant challenge. Parents may remember their own real or imagined material deprivation as children; in turn, they may overcompensate, undermining their child's own independence and self-competence. Parents are most generous when they expect their children to "work for what they get." Frequent, lavish gifts teach children nothing about self-reliance, create jealousy among peers, and develop "spoiled brats." There are blessings in *doing without,* and having worked hard to pay my own college education, I have doubts about the wisdom of large trust funds for children's education.

The professional family is highly visible in small cities and towns, and personal privacy diminishes. When we are in a public place such as a restaurant, my wife often remarks, "I think we are being watched." Sure enough, I soon spy someone whom I have seen professionally. It is the old fishbowl feeling.

The Time Crunch

A major stress on the family of a professional is time. Some professionals must put in longer hours than a 40-hour work week; they may always be "on call." The particular profession may demand a high level of expertise, decisions may affect the welfare of many people, and frequently there are no easy answers. "Burn out" may result; then the professional feels irritable and overwhelmed, and loses the pleasure previously enjoyed in work. The family is deprived of the attentive presence, commitment, and love of this parent, who feels empty and has little to give. The parent promises to go on a picnic with the rest of the family, but declines at the last minute; "I am sorry, but something unexpected came up." Knowing when to say no to one's family is difficult. Equally important is knowing when to say no to pleas for help from others, especially after regular hours. Not all "emergencies" are truly emergencies.

If the professional parent is unable or unwilling to limit time demands and is consistently unavailable, family members become resentful toward the parent or the profession itself. Such resentment may be puzzling—the more "Big Shot" serves the clients, the worse things seem to go at home. Gradually, then, the professional parent unconsciously devotes more time to the office where respect and admiration flow freely! To prevent this, both parents need to support each other emotionally and help the children feel each parent has equally important responsibilities to carry out. Such competition for loyalty is a continuing tension which is never satisfactorily resolved, just as friendship or marriage itself are never static. Good communication one day may evaporate the next. One can only resolve to be faithful to the best of one's ability, to the high calling of both the profession and the family.

"Medicine," allegedly, "is like a jealous mistress." The implication is that one must make a difficult choice: either marry one's work or give it up. This is a fallacy. Professionals do not have to choose between work or family; they can devote themselves to work *and* family. Young children, compared to older children, need more parental nurture. This is often just the time when the professional is completing his or her training and professional identity is beginning to solidify. Unfortunately, the greatest demand for family attention often comes at the same time when the pressures of making it in a profession are at their peak.

Frequent, brief vacations, with and without the children, should be creatively planned. For young children, anticipating an evening ice-cream spree when the whole family is together can mean ecstasy. Licking and slurping burgundy cherry and lemon custard, the children would rather eat than talk. Not so the parents, who savor the brief reprieve from prattle.

There is the delight of many choices: perhaps a walk through the park with the whole family; or parents might engage in separate activities with older and younger children; even a lop-sided split encourages deeper ties. The usually unavailable parent might take all the children for rides on the bumper cars, do errands with them, or devote attention to only the one who needs special attention that day. Adolescents may yawn out of boredom when the busy one proudly announces the family options for the day off. Yet, when the timing is just right, the shared experiences will live in memories forever.

Fortunately, many professional people have flexible time schedules. Recently my daughter Lesley was Peter Pan in a Friday afternoon school performance. Not many parents employed on an hourly basis were able to attend. I was able to block out time in advance to attend. Her grins of pleasure as we entered the gymnasium were adequate proof that the special planning was worth it. I also attend parent-teacher conferences each time, if possible. Benjy, our nursery schooler, gets special attention from Dr. Seuss when I come home for lunch breaks. However, I have learned not to drop in hastily just for food; if that is my sole intention, it is better to stay away!

Professional Papas and Mamas

Professional parents comprise a very select group, having survived college and the rigors of further professional training. Combining high intelligence (hopefully), perseverance, and other favorable circumstances, they have succeeded. In some families, both parents have careers. Being better educated does not make one a better parent, although it is correlated with a greater use of reason than physical punishment in the discipline of children. However, the children of professionals may not share these talents and favorable personality attributes.

Parental expectations may clash with what the child is "cut out" to be. Being average is healthy; parents need to take pride in the average achievements of their children. Although parents may deny they are exposing their children to excessively high expectations, I often see nervous mothers and fathers occupied with small failures in their children's development. Or they may enroll their youngsters in numerous activities, causing sensory overload and performance anxiety.

Ideally, the children of professionals benefit from increased intellectual and aesthetic stimulation and hopefully see the joys of service to others. They may, however, develop a self-centered pursuit of fame, money, or the desire to have power over others, especially if that is the motivating force in their parents' careers.

Fathers have in the past usually been the professionals. Happily, professions are now more accessible to women, and

---

Why I Switched to Banking

By J. B. Miller, Jr.

During the 1960s, when I was a college student, there was a great deal of emphasis placed on selecting a profession which would directly contribute to healing the social ills that exist in our society. Because of some of these pressures, I chose to become a high school history teacher. My aim was to stimulate students to think about the issues, just as several of my teachers had done for me.

I taught for one year and was not a success. I was such a failure that I decided to move back to the security of my hometown where I could be among family and friends.

My father, being a rather practical person, thought I should seek employment and suggested that I apply for a job at a bank. I rebelled at that idea since I knew my socially aware friends would think I had sold out to the establishment. But I was desperate. I had bills to pay; besides, my friends were far from Sarasota in places like Washington, D.C., Flint, Lancaster, and New York. They could provide no financial assistance.

Being a "closet" business and finance student (I had taken a few finance courses when my friends weren't looking), I did not have a strong academic background for banking. But I was able to find employment with a banker who felt I had potential.

At first the entry level position made few demands—be at work by 8:30 and leave by 5:30. However, with each promotion the time demands became more intense.

some training programs are tailored to meet the special needs of mothers with small children. Even in medicine, where training has traditionally been rigidly structured, women physicians may study part time, and practice part days while caring for their families. Deciding when to start a family becomes a matter of juggling many factors for a couple, including age, income, emotional readiness, competing time priorities, and so forth.

What about working professional mothers? Are their children deprived? Not necessarily so. If children are provided with excellent substitute care, the potentially harmful effects of parental absences are reduced, if not completely canceled. A

Now there are demands on each minute. During intensely demanding periods, church and family life take a backseat to my profession. I hurt during these times because my close relationships suffer. My body suffers as well. There isn't always time for lunch, and dinner may be a quick drive-through at McDonalds.

The pressure to become a competent banker in the eyes of my peers gives me the energy to continue. Being respected by my colleagues is important to me, since they are the only ones capable of assessing my performance.

Persons within the congregation do not always seem to understand my professional pressures. It is easy for them to sympathize with a medical doctor who is unable to attend a meeting because of an emergency, but they are less considerate when another professional is unable to attend a church function because of career demands.

If I am to perform to my optimum, there are times when the demands of my profession take precedence over those of church and family. I need to judge when the choice to put the profession first will not have a lasting negative impact on my relationships within these groups. The risk of making a wrong decision is high.

During demanding times I need my church and family as a caring community to reach out and be supportive because it is through my profession that I gain a portion of my identity and a tremendous feeling of accomplishment.

professionally employed mother, who finds her work stimulating and fulfilling, has more to give emotionally to her children than one who is angry about "being at home." However, such positive advantages may be eliminated if the husband or children are critical of her employment. Children of working professional mothers may have a weaker attachment to their mothers than children whose mothers are full-time care givers. This is especially true if the mothers began working when their children were infants.

If a mother has started her career while the children are preschoolers, full-time substitute care becomes imperative. If such substitute care is provided daily by the same person, which is desirable, the children may develop a very close attachment to this substitute "mother" that rivals in strength the tie between child and mother. This is one of the trade-offs families make, but perhaps preventive measures can be taken. Brofenbrenner (1973) writes that day-care and preschool centers should be located near places of business, so that during coffee breaks and lunch hours people could visit their kids.

For centuries mothers have been the primary care givers, but fatherhood is finally being studied and, especially in recent years, heralded. Fathers can, and should be, affectionate, nurturers of their children. In some families the child's emotional bond may be stronger to the father than to the mother. Therefore, professionally employed fathers should not underestimate the profound healthy impact they can have on their children's growth and development, even though the time of actual contact may be less, compared to mothers.

An increasing number of families are childless, which reduces the complexity of role conflicts and eliminates the potential for parental deprivation. Professional families often are more mobile than others. On the positive side, such moves because of work or training opportunities provide the family with awareness of different cultures and lifestyles and may be quite stimulating.

A potential move should be approached deliberately and

cautiously. Each family member has an opinion, but the decision
to pull up roots remains an adult one. On the negative side, of
course, is the jeopardy that frequent moves puts on each family
member's sense of stability and security. Preschool children may
be affected less, since their environment is primarily homebound.

Children may be indirectly affected by a move. Both parents
may adapt poorly to moves and become tense, irritable, and
lonely. Or one parent may resent the move. If so, they may become more critical and punitive toward their children. Parents
who are lonely in the new community may create an excessively
dependent relationship with their children. Moves often prevent
or disrupt close family ties to grandparents who can provide the
parents and children with a sense of interrelatedness and an
awareness of aging. But letters are cheap and mobile families can
adopt friendly, available, elderly neighbors as substitute
grandparents.

Unprofessional at Home

What *role* does the professional parent's career play at
home? Preferably none. At home, mother the doctor or father
the teacher is simply a parent and a spouse. I lose patience with
my children despite the fact that my daily professional work involves counseling parents in distress who lose patience with their
children! In the family setting, the professional parent needs to be
human, imperfect, and on a par with the other parent. He or she
must be vulnerable and subject to criticism. The additional skill
and expertise that she or he possesses distorts family functioning
if this parent plays a special role, becomes detached from the
family, and expects the other parent to assume the bulk of the
child rearing. If a busy parent waltzes in after a heavy day at the
office, expecting to be waited on or to be treated with homage,
conflict is inevitable. The remaining family members need to
sense they are as important as the career of the professional
parent.

Although professional skills must be updated to prevent
obsolescence, no substitute for the family has yet been invented.

Here love, responsibility, and the joy of hard work are first taught. Healthy self-esteem and a sense of belonging are best developed in one's family of origin. The children see daily how love and anger are demonstrated and how resentment and conflict can be channeled into creative, deeper relationships without destroying commitment. There is no magic formula for instilling Christian values; the almost infinite encounters children witness in the working out of human relationships are their teachers. Parents who are affectionate *and* authoritative (not authoritarian) most successfully instill their own values in their young.

"Daddy, but what do you do at your office?" Lesley, age 8, may ask. How can I adequately explain to her the nature of my daily work? I tell her, "I am a doctor. I teach other doctors about how to help children. I help children who feel sad, unhappy, and angry, or who do not get along with their parents." She knows about sadness, about being angry. We talk about how she felt angry at me or my wife for being "mean" yesterday, or how she knows Benjy "hates" her, and how she got over it, and how some children and parents cannot get over their feelings and may need professional help. But to show my family members exactly what I do when I'm working is impossible. My professional ethics demand confidentiality, and my work goes on behind closed doors. I take my children to my office sometimes on weekends, so they can see one of the many settings in which I work. They see my books, the office furniture, the toys the children play with, and they delight in playing with my dictaphone.

There are harder questions like, "Why do you go to so many meetings, daddy?" I try to answer. I *think* I know the reasons. But do my wife and children genuinely accept them? Perhaps they have a conception of father-husband as "someone who is gone a lot." Our time together becomes more precious before and after business trips. Souvenirs, hastily plucked from airport concession stands while I catch an airplane home, seem an artificial and inadequate Band-Aid for making separations less damaging. As I write this, I have just returned home from a weekend in Chicago, spending long hours with psychiatrists debating esoteric problems within the profession. I walk in the door, happy to be home, trying to tell my wife about the trip. Benjamin, age 4, keeps kissing me. My attempts to gaze past him to keep eye contact with my wife, as I report how my colleagues and I prevented disaster for the profession, become more difficult. Benjy "pecks" me more emphatically. I finally perceive his needs and carry him in my arms to another room. We are all alone; we talk together, perhaps about Superman's latest exploits; he is pleased and I am touched by the closeness. Benjamin needed to be special that moment, having me all to himself. Adult matters will wait.

More clearly visible to my children and wife is my life at home. Benjamin and Lesley watch me put up a shelf; better yet, I start the nail and let them finish, despite the unplanned "antiqued" effect on the wood as the hammer glances off target. I grit my teeth. My professional standards—of needing to perform efficiently, rapidly, and without error—must be bridled. Children learn by doing, and mine will too if I don't stand in their way. My wife gave me a poster for my office door, reading, "Of course children get in your way, but where are you going?" Every professional must answer this question. "The only really important time in our lives is the time we waste with those we love" (Saint Exupery, 1943).

CHAPTER NINE

The Impact of Professionalism on Congregations

By Sheldon W. Burkhalter

Then and Now

The process of professionalization and specialization has gradually accelerated in North American society for the past century, but our churches were little affected by it until three or four decades ago. Ever since, we have been galloping to catch up.

Several decades ago the typical congregation consisted primarily of families who farmed or operated farm-related small businesses. Ethnic heritage and the church community were the most important molders of beliefs, values, and lifestyle. Long-distance travel was rare. Education consisted of what one gained from home and the country school. Life had been this way for several centuries.

The local congregation was the most important and consistent social link with the past. It gathered weekly or biweekly in the meetinghouse for preaching, Sunday school instruction, and observance of the ordinances of baptism and communion. Congregational structure was very simple: a team of preachers and deacons ministered the Word and the ordinances, trustees maintained the meetinghouse, and superintendents organized Sunday school. Most importantly, all these leaders had grown up in the congregation where they served, had no formal training for their leadership task, and received little or no payment from the church. Occasional revival meetings were the only marked diversion from this pattern when a *visiting* preacher came and a love offering was lifted for his ministry.

Since World War II there are significant changes in our congregations and it is clear that the increase of diverse professions and specialization among our members has been one of the leading forces. Instead of the uniformity of the small farming enterprise, congregational members today are skilled laborers, teachers, doctors, nurses, psychologists, social workers, researchers, secretaries, business and industrial workers, clerks, and managers. While not all of these would be strictly defined as "professional," most do require some form of special training. A further change is that many women have also moved into the job market. These factors mark substantial shifts in our congregational life in just one generation.

The impact of this new diversity in our membership has been most noticeable in the way we organize our life together. We form church councils and numerous committees to run the many programs of the church. This development has grown in part out of our increased awareness of our needs in a complex world, but also from our belief that through organizations we can do things in a better way. We have committees for stewardship, nurture, fellowship, worship, and witness, as well as for nursery care, youth ministry, singles, family life, and senior members.

Another noticeable change in recent decades has been the way we call and support congregational leaders—now labeled "pastors"—along with how we define their role. Instead of looking within the membership, we usually call a pastor from another congregation. Since our members are more highly educated, we expect the pastor to be trained for his task as well. Pastors' salaries are provided and job descriptions written. This shift to salaried pastors requires increased financial support from the congregation; as a result, most churches adopt the most realistically "affordable" single pastor model of leadership, thus losing or significantly altering the shared ministry approach of the traditional "bench" pattern of bishops, ministers, and deacons.

Evaluating the Change

This shift to a more highly organized congregational structure, and to employing one trained and salaried pastor from outside the congregation, is the result of increased professionalization, specialization, and diversification among the members of our congregations. In many ways it has been a natural and reasonable response to our needs. And it appeared to us to work well in thriving Protestant churches. We have lived with this model long enough to evaluate some of its strengths and weaknesses.

On the positive side, our organized church life, with its committees and programs, has caused us to take a serious look at spiritual gifts. In order to fill offices and meet needs in the congregation, many members ask, "What are my gifts?" and "What are your gifts for building up the body of Christ?" The church is encouraging and training persons for the meaningful exercise of their gifts. The New Testament teaching on the church as a body possessing many *charismata* (grace gifts) focuses upon *diversity, variety,* and *specialization* for the purpose of unifying and building up the body of Christ. Community thrives where individuals function in many interdependent special assignments in an orderly fashion.

The training of pastors has also been a necessary and helpful change in the church. Formerly church leaders learned primarily by doing and by apprenticeship under more experienced leaders. However, our increasingly seductive and complex society makes it ever more important for pastors to be formally trained in Bible, theology, education, and counseling. The church has recognized this need by establishing and supporting colleges, seminaries, and local apprenticeship programs for training pastors.

Seven Concerns

While the increased focus upon spiritual gifts and the training of pastors is a happy development, increased professionalism, specialization, and diversification among our members has led us to function in ways that are also a cause for concern. We can unknowingly adopt patterns that weaken our life together. The following statements heard in many of our congregations illustrate the negative impact of professionalism on congregational life.

The *first* statement is the often heard response of one who has been asked by the church to serve in a particular task: "I'm not professional enough." This person often suggests that "others are more capable," fearing he or she will not do as well as someone else or will fail. Sometimes congregations are overly critical and thus discourage members from trying new opportunities. But the church's call should be seriously considered because careful thought and prayer have usually gone into such requests; someone is apparently confident that the person being asked can do it. Surely within the caring community one ought to be free to take the risk of trying out new tasks. This is one way new capabilities are discovered.

The *second* statement I have often heard from committees who make appointments: "She was trained to do that for her job, so she ought to be able to do it well in the church." It is natural to assume that the trained accountant would make a capable congregational treasurer, the contractor a good trustee, and the school teacher an effective Sunday school teacher. But some members prefer their involvement in the congregation to be a change from what they do five days a week; new challenges sometimes tap fresh energy. To be sure, professional know-how can be helpful when serving in some functions of the church. Yet the main criteria for meeting needs in the congregation is spiritual preparedness: giftedness, commitment, and availability.

The *third* statement is often heard from the professional: "This is the way it's done in my work so we ought to do the same here in church." Such statements are sometimes true, but the congregation is not just a business venture or another institution in society. Methodology in a congregation may need to be quite different from a secular organization. For example, a pastor who tries to lead like a corporate executive is headed for serious conflict. On the other hand, sound management principles and counseling techniques, when faithfully tested by the Scriptures, can be helpful in the church. The tendency in our professionalized world is to think more in psychological and political terms than in biblical ones. The caution here is that methods which work very well in the professional world should not be transferred uncritically into the church.

A *fourth* statement goes like this: "I don't have time to help in the church because my job keeps me too busy." Surely one's profession can be considered a most important context from which Christian service is done. Yet our economically competitive society has increasingly taken persons away from their family and church. A few decades ago only men felt this pressure. Now women and young people have become less available to the church because they also have the ready excuse, "I have a job." Furthermore, complex vacation schedules and monotonous work fosters the retreating of members to the mountains or the shore on weekends. This is causing great problems for the cohesiveness of local congregations.

Fifth, we sometimes hear the complaint: "This church is run by the well educated." In many congregations professionals, because of their training and abilities to articulate their views, are most able to influence congregational policy and decisions. Further, the wide diversity of educational backgrounds and occupations results in the formation of subgroups in the congregation, each with their own language, interests, and values. While all members need to work at breaking down these walls, professionals especially can help by being more sensitive to and encouraging of those who feel less able to express their ideas and to lead in congregational projects.

The *sixth* statement relates especially to when a trained pastor is called from outside the congregation: "Now that we have a trained pastor, we can do all those things other churches do successfully." Highly unrealistic expectations are often placed on the trained pastor: "We can now count on biblical and inspirational sermons *every* Sunday." "The pastor's counseling can save my daughter's marriage." "I will not only gain a warm personal friend but take pride in introducing my pastor to my non-Christian neighbor." "The church budget will surely prosper now." Just as Marcus Welby does not exist, neither does such a pastor.

The cause of unrealistic expectations varies from one congregation to another. One source is the mystique with which many professionals operate. Many view professors, and especially doctors, with almost reverential esteem. Pastors are also put on a pedestal and thought to have a special calling from God.

A further source of unrealistic expectations for pastors comes in the transition from the "homegrown" pastor to the calling of a theologically educated pastor from outside the congregation. If the homegrown ones did well without salary and training, then the new pastor ought to do much better. However, the transition may be difficult. One possible explanation is that when the former pastor was called from within the congregation, his capabilities were already well known; therefore, false hopes never developed. Especially important is the fact that he was highly trusted for his ability to lead the congregation. His past relationship with the members enabled him to speak their language. Furthermore, in the older pattern, a team of several ministers served together giving every member the sense that "God might call me to their position too." Often the congregational community was *in itself* all the "pastoral care" that was needed. These dynamics usually provided a strong base for pastoral support.

"Educated" pastors from outside the congregation usually are capable interpreters of the Bible and knowledgeable in church history, pastoral counseling, and church administration. However, this training is only part of what many congregations expect of a pastor. They also want a personal relationship with him. This takes considerable time for an outside person to cultivate; I suspect that it can never develop to the degree that the homegrown pastor experienced. When expectations are not met, congregations begin to feel that the pastor does not understand them while the pastor himself feels isolated; this may be further compounded by the fact that he may be serving alone with no one in the congregation to turn to for support.

A *seventh* statement reflecting a negative impact of professionalism also relates to the role of the pastor: "The pastor is paid to preach, counsel, and visit, so I don't see why my help is needed." This comment reflects a passive pew-sitter waiting to be recharged for the week ahead. Ministry is thus professionalized or limited to only a few and no longer the shared responsibility of the whole church community.

Choosing a Church

By José M. Ortiz

José M. Ortiz has a doctor of ministry degree from McCormick Seminary in Chicago and is heading back to school to take more courses in administration. He is a voracious reader of contemporary poetry, business theory, theology, and political commentary. He works as associate general secretary for Latin concerns for the Mennonite Church. His chosen congregation: The Church of the Good Shepherd in Goshen, Indiana, a Hispanic group of about 100 people whose pastor has a sixth-grade education.

He spoke with the editors about his understanding of education and the effect degrees should have on selecting one's faith community:

Because you're academically successful doesn't mean you have to move away from those you grew up with. We must develop a broader understanding of education. It's the capacity to live along with your peers, *and* the people you grew up with. It's learning to live with those tensions.

Once you get your education, it's easy to become a product for exportation rather than consumption. It's tempting to move away. But that's just another kind of brain drain. If with my presence I can support the people I grew up with in my church, that's important. That's why I hang around. That way I can demonstrate a different kind of education. You *can* model it.

I've made a commitment to my congregation. To see someone bloom and develop—that's growth for them and for me. Simple people have so many sides to their faith. It's a challenge.

I pray with the pastor. I feed in ideas. We have a good rapport. Instead of nice, soft-spoken sermons, you discipline yourself to be close to your people. It's a challenge in a whole other way.

Mid-course Correctives

Professionalism in itself is not wrong; it is, like the emotion of anger, neutral. It depends on what we do with professionalism that determines whether it is to be a creative urge for Christian service or a destructive force of congregational disintegration.

Of *first* importance is the rediscovery of the church community as the center of our lives. Individualism suggests that self, one's family, and occupation are at the core of personal identity. When asked, "Who are you?" we answer with our name, family, and job. However, the New Testament teaches that as the people of God we are solely concerned with the lordship of the crucified Jesus. Our fullest identity is found in relationship with Christ and his community. With Jesus and the faith community at our core, we are then called to serve in the broader setting in which we find ourselves, namely in our biological family, our occupation, and "our world." The way we function in our professions, therefore, needs to come under a vigorous biblical critique. Even for those in the institutions of the church, such as schools and retirement communities, the local congregation is the primary fellowship and the base from which God's will is discovered. When we fail to live from the center of our being—relationship to Christ and Christian fellowship—we become less than Christian and we lose community.

Second, we need to recover a biblical understanding of service. Central to our response to Christ is *diakonia,* the Greek word for service or ministry. Jesus supremely exemplified *diakonia* in his earthly ministry: "I am among you as one who serves" (Luke 22:24-27; cf. Mark 10:42-45). Paul roots *diakonia* in the congregation; it is the gift or work of the Holy Spirit (1 Corinthians 12:4-7). Significantly, Paul avoids the terms office, vocation, occupation, or function; instead there are "varieties of service." The focus of the Spirit's gifting is thus not upon office or profession but upon how we live our life together. Jürgen Moltmann, (1978) prominent German theologian at the University of Tübingen, said, ". . . before the Christian community begins to practice diakonal service toward others, it must be within itself a caring community. The Christian community is already within itself a diakonal community or it is neither a community nor Christian.... The ordinary laws of social stratification and the struggle for recognition and for power end at the point where members begin to serve one another with their best efforts and together all live out the servanthood of Jesus."

Third, this *diakonia* is not simply the ministry of a select few in the congregation; all members are called to ministry. In the Old Testament the Spirit of God rested only upon prophets, priests, and kings, but in the new covenant the Holy Spirit energizes the whole people of God: men and women, young and old, Jews and Gentiles, slaves and free (Acts 2:17; Galations 3:28; 1 Corinthians 12:13ff.). A serious departure from biblical Christianity occurs when *diakonia* is hired or "professionalized" and made the calling of only a few, like pastors and missionaries.

Sometimes pastors, in an autocratic grasp for power, usurp functions belonging to the members. In many congregations ministry is delegated to the pastor (often one person serving alone in the congregation) who is expected to preach, teach, counsel, administer, raise funds, evangelize, and visit, all with equal excellence. Instead of members being active servants, they become the objects of service and thus assume less responsibility for the lives of others or even for their own. They want to be handed beliefs and values rather than personally searching for and claiming them. The result is that members become ever more passive and the congregation ceases being a community.

To prevent this sickness, congregations need to focus upon the discovery and the exercise of spiritual gifts so that each member becomes an active participant in the church's ministry. Leadership, which must be shared, has the responsibility of providing direction for the congregation without usurping the personal initiative and accountability of the individual members. When leadership persons exercise their particular gifts, they do so as servants calling all others to service in the interrelatedness of the whole congregation. Community thrives where there is diversity, special assignments, and interdependence.

Elders with their roots in the congregation could particularly assume more of what is commonly called "pastoral care" and "church administration," freeing pastors to offer more from their special training in biblical interpretation and counseling. The New Testament pattern of elders serving alongside the more mobile ministries of pastors like Timothy, Titus, Priscilla, and Aquila could become a useful model for us.

As professionals and specialists take their place among the rest, the whole congregation can be a serving and caring community. The unique gifts and special training of the professional enhances life together; with their help, the church's corporate mission to the world can be expanded. How we place ourselves in the midst of the Christian community is the crux of the matter.

CHAPTER TEN

The Impact of Professionalism on Pastors

By Frank Ward

An Almost Professional Pastor's Diary

Waiting for a meeting to begin this morning, I asked my friend Judy, a member of our congregation, "What's your definition of a professional?"

Her response was immediate. "Someone who competes for money instead of just for fun or excitement." Judy is something of a jock.

"No," I said, "what I mean is, what's your definition of a professional other than a professional athlete—you know, like a doctor or lawyer."

"Oh," she said. "Well—I don't know—I guess it's a person who works at a profession rather than a regular job." Before I could comment she went on. "I know, now you're going to ask me to define 'profession' and 'regular job.' "

"Well," I suggested, "before you do, do you consider *me* a professional?"

"You?" she asked. "I never really thought about it. I guess I do in some ways and I don't in others. Does that help?"

*   *   *

This morning I walked into the church wearing a sport coat and tie (and the other stuff that goes with them, naturally).

"Hey," Ruby, the Nutrition Site supervisor yelled, "Where are you going? To a funeral?"

"No," I said, "I'm just going to be around the church all day. Why?"

"Well," she said, "I don't usually see you wearing a coat and tie unless it's Sunday, honey."

I straightened my tie. "I've been reading some excerpts from the book, *Dress for Success,* and I wanted to see if I can get more authority and respect around here."

Ruby slapped her thigh and laughed. "Honey, if it's respect you want, you ain't gonna earn it by wearing a coat and a tie. That's like skinning a cat with a toothbrush!"

Dress for Success says that my authority and power are undercut if I don't wear the proper suit. Maybe I don't want that kind of power anyway. So I'll go without a tie and "make myself of no reputation," as the apostle Paul says.

But there's another side to the problem. If I give up my tie and wear jeans, I gain respect and power with another sizable group in our congregation: the simple, lifestyle gang. They think it's great when I wear jeans and T-shirts. Maybe I should write my own book and call it, *Dress and Undress for Success.*

*   *   *

Judy also says a professional is "someone who doesn't dirty his or her hands." "Doctors and nurses do," I argued.

"That's different," she replied, "blood and stuff don't count as dirt. They're still professional people even if they have to wash their hands a lot."

This afternoon Ruby came up to my office to tell me that the ladies' toilet was stopped up again. "Can you fix it, honey?" she asked.

Why not? I was getting tired of filling out a statistics form, so we found the plunger. Luckily, it wasn't bad and I got it unclogged with little trouble.

Until Allen found out about it. "Frank," he said, "it just isn't right that you go around fixing toilets and electrical switches and things."

"Why not?" I asked.

"Well, it isn't the right kind of image for you to have," he said. "It isn't professional." (Allen even has his high school diploma hanging in his office.)

"I don't really mind doing it once in a while," I said. "It saves a $30 bill from the plumber."

"That's not the point," Allen responded.

Oh well, I lost him—but I won Ruby. The trouble is I don't know what the score really is.

*   *   *

Some people clearly don't pay attention to me unless they can think of me as a professional. I remember Mrs. Miller in my first pastorate who always introduced me to influential friends as "Doctor Ward" or "the Reverend Frank Ward." I always was tempted to respond with, "Just call me Frankie."

But another group won't listen to me unless they perceive me as a nonprofessional. Should I play the game? Do I really want authority? (Why are management skills workshops so popular with ministers right now? I get two or three notices in the mail each week.) Okay, I don't want to lord it over people, but I do want them to give fair consideration to what I say, both from the pulpit and in committees.

Another question. Do I give as much consideration to the ideas of nonprofessional people in the congregation as I do to those of the professionals? To the ideas of the less affluent as well as those of the more affluent? Do I automatically attach more worth to some than to others? Better think about that, Frank.

*   *   *

Yesterday I had some business with Greg, another minister with whom (I confess) I associate as little as possible. Greg is "CPE" (that's Clinical Pastoral Education) from his toenails to his beret. One hundred and one percent. He fairly oozes care and concern, and is obviously distraught if you don't give him at least one opportunity during each visit to practice his counseling craft on you.

His secretary, who's been at the church longer than Greg has, was complaining to me before he came in.

"I made a mistake on the bulletin last week," she said, "so I told him about it to find out if I should do it over. But, instead, he kept telling me what a 'really marvelous' job I had done on the other page. Finally I told him flat out, 'Look, you don't have to go through all this just because you're going to ask me to do it over. Just *tell* me!' "

"He cares more about caring," she said, "than he cares about people."

Professionals may not fool people as much as they think. Uneducated, hurting, drunk, or whatever—people have an uncanny ability to know when they are genuinely cared for and loved. I wonder if CPE Greg believes that. Do I? Judy says just because everybody needs professionals doesn't mean they really trust them.

*   *   *

I looked into the eyes of a dying boy last night and I was scared. An automobile accident, a midnight call, a boy (dying, they said) wanting to be anointed. I'd never done it before, so I had to borrow oil from a nurse.

Why was I scared? Because he was just a kid? Because he was exactly my son's age? Because his parents were afraid they were going to lose him? Because I didn't know how to help him and couldn't remember a single line from a dozen books I'd read on ministering to the dying? Because I'd never looked into the eyes of a dying boy before?

Answer: yes. And probably "yes" to another dozen reasons I haven't even begun to ferret out yet and maybe never will.

Judy says a professional is well-trained and always knows what to do in any situation. "Or pretends to," she adds.

After they took the boy to the operating room, his parents sat down and began to cry. The next thing I knew, I was crying too.

*   *   *

Does the grace and love of God operate in spite of me? To what degree? Suppose I were a charlatan and put on a priest's collar and walked around a hospital blessing people and praying for them? I wonder what would happen?

Judy says a professional is trained in a specific body of knowledge, passes some kind of licensing examination, keeps his or her cool, has the situation under control, always knows what to do, and has the answers. "Never admit you don't know if you want to keep your professional image," she says.

But is that what I'm called to do as a pastor? I don't even need to stand behind one of those massive, majestic pulpits (some of them look like parapets on a castle wall from which you shoot your arrows and darts on the enemy below) to discover myself chock full of sagacious answers bursting to be dispensed.

There are times when I'm convinced that my task as a minister is helping people formulate questions, to clarify and sharpen them. Then together as a congregation we work toward finding the answers.

Do I help people in my congregation best when I operate out of a stance (the military term is "posture") of strength, power, authority, wisdom—a stance that is over against theirs more often than not—or when I take a position of weakness? Isn't that when I really stand *with* people?

Maybe I shouldn't worry because I cried with those parents. Jesus once cried for a whole city.

* * *

I've been trained. I've been examined and approved for ordination (though I doubt, if I went back and applied now, that my answers would be accepted). I know the jargon—and probably use it too frequently. I've got a title and a couple of degrees. I must be a professional! My physician, who knows I'm a minister, generously offered me a half price deal for some treatment I had received from him. When I said I didn't feel comfortable accepting that, he thought for a minute. "All right," he suggested, "I'll just take ten percent off the bill. That's my standard discount for all professional people."

I understand the relationship a physician or lawyer has with a patient or client. But it's impossible for me to keep that same kind of distance. Members don't come to see me only in circumstances of need. I visit them, work with them, study with them, play with them, argue with them (sometimes I win and sometimes I lose), eat with them, and share their joys as well as their sorrows.

*   *   *

More thoughts on the ultimate question. Judy and I were driving together to a meeting yesterday.

"What did you ever decide?" she asked me.

"About what?" was my astute response.

"You know—are you or aren't you a professional?"

"That's absolutely correct," I said.

She laughed. "Does it depress you that you can't arrive at a clear, precise answer?"

"No, not really," I said. "I've learned how to handle insecurity and lack of respect and all that."

"Good," she said. "And to help you feel better, I'll treat you to lunch."

That Judy is one fine woman. She really knows how to deal with ultimate questions.

Dilemmas of Professionalism

CHAPTER ELEVEN

Manufacturing Need and Mystery

By Donald B. Kraybill

Needy Professionals

The *Chicago Tribune* recently carried a half-page advertisement with a picture of a large computer-like machine. The bold lettering at the top of the ad read:

> If you are ill or injured there is only *one* place in Illinois where your tests can be made on the latest CT scanning equipment.

My first reaction was to ask myself whether or not I was ill or injured. Certainly I have been both ill and injured at various times throughout my life, although I am feeling quite fine at the moment. But the heading on this ad raises some questions and doubts about my current good health. Since this is the *only* place to get the most advanced tests that are sensitive to any abnormalities in my body, and since I have never been to this place— never even heard of the Skokie Valley Computed Tomography Centre—maybe I am ill or injured and do not even know it. Perhaps the older outdated computerized detectors at my local hospital missed something. In fact, I never even heard of tomography before—maybe I'm infected with a new disease and don't even know it.

Suddenly I have a need. I might have a latent disease. So in the name of preventive medicine, bodily stewardship, and good common sense, I decide to check this thing out. At least if I don't have anything, I'll have peace of mind and the assurance of knowing that I've been scanned by the greatest scanner of all time. But as I pack my bags and head toward Skokie Valley, I begin to wonder if I really do need this scan. Might it be that scanners need people so they try to convince them that they ought to be scanned? Since I don't have a need to help them meet their needs, I dump my bags back in the closet and stay home.

Irony penetrates the term "need" in the personal service professions—those professions whose major function is to bring about a change in the body, personality, or attitudes of the clients. Clients are usually thought of as the needy ones with deficiencies or maladies which they bring to the professional for treatment. Prior to treatment the professionals decide whether or not the client does have a need—for the client may not know. Their need is labeled and a remedy is prescribed which usually involves active intervention by the professional provider. Finally, the professional who defined, labeled, prescribed treatment, and treated the need, decides whether or not the treatment has effectively eradicated the need. The underlying assumption is that the client is not qualified to determine whether or not the need has been satisfied.

The whole framework of professional care assumes that it is the clients or students who are the needy. In fact, the professional providers are often the "needy" ones, however. They must have clients to maintain their job and income and "cases" to support and feed their economic structures. Anyone working with human service agencies can testify to many interagency skirmishes over clients; for example, "If we can't keep our quota of clients, our funding will go." So what appears as "service to the needy client," too often is a pleasant mask that covers up the greedy face of a very hungry economic system fighting for its survival. John McKnight (1977) says, "Behind the mask is simply the servicer, his systems, techniques, and technologies—a business in need of markets, an economy seeking new growth potential, professionals in need of an income." In modern societies dominated by service economies, the average citizens lose their power to define their own needs.

Artificial Needs

Personal needs are artificially created and manufactured by professionals who need clients. Service economies thrive on manufacturing personal deficiencies and inadequacies to fuel their systems. The comic extreme of such a "service society" is one in which neighbors discover that their own bread and butter—usually done in the name of professionalized love—comes from meeting the artificial needs and deficiencies that they have created in each other. Individuals need death counseling because they don't know how to die, they need career management counseling because they don't know what they can do, and they need sex therapy because they don't know how to make love! So neighbors end up serving the artificial deficiencies that they have created in each other.

The artificial need is manufactured by professional systems to ensure their own economic survival. The fabrication of deficiencies is often accelerated by technological innovation, competition from other providers, and the maintenance of personal income in the face of ambiguous need. Mushrooming advances in technology create enormous need, both real and imagined. One feels an almost ethical obligation to use these wonderful, shiny new toys. It seems like such a shame to spend millions of dollars in the research and development of the latest scanner and then not use it. A recent study of open-heart surgery in California pointed out that 70 percent of the California hospitals were below the federal standards of minimal use (200 operations per year). The problem is that hospitals under the federal standards had much higher death rates because of their inexperience. All the hospitals wanted the prestige associated with open-heart surgery. With federal pressure to increase the number of operations per year, artificial need must be created. Somehow people will need to be convinced that they need more open-heart surgery so that the technological toys don't sit idly by.

Competition from other professional providers also produces artificial need. Colleges and universities are facing shrinking enrollments. They desperately need clients to feed their hungry systems. Since there is a severe limit to the number of college-age students, "educational need" is being created among a new group of potential students. Adults who have not completed college are informed that they can "find themselves," "develop their potential," "achieve their goals," and "maximize skills" in programs of "lifelong" learning. Such promotion of adult and continuing education programs creates the illusion that such adults have needs or deficiencies. It implies that they haven't "found themselves yet" and "haven't developed to their potential." In other words, the college would like them to take courses for the rest of their lives so the school doesn't have to lay off any professors.

When need is ambiguous it can often be made urgent and real. The dentist suggests that an orthodontist ought to examine the development of a particular tooth in a child's mouth. The unwary parent is not sure whether an orthodontist is needed or not. But after the examination there is no doubt; an orthodontist is a must. The child's bite is off a fraction of an inch, some teeth are tilted slightly in the wrong direction, there is space between other teeth in the front, another tooth yet in the gum isn't pointed in the right direction, and there's still another one that's crowded. These are grave and serious problems. Worse yet, if not attended to, they will produce even greater trouble. The child definitely needs an orthodontist. The need is so persuasive that a doubting parent is embarrassed to even ask if this is really necessary. Orthodontic treatment would result in a more aesthetically appealing mouth, but how necessary is it?

That these technical adjustments *can* be done virtually results in a moral obligation that they *ought* to be done. To doubt their need is a sin of the highest order in a professionalized society. The creation of this need today is strong and subtle, for parents want to provide the best for their children. Having their child's faulty mouth repaired is the least they can do to show their fundamental identity as good and caring parents. Such appealing definitions of need are hard to ignore.

Lest anyone think this is an unfair assault on orthodontists, be aware that the orthodontist's prescription bears a striking resemblence to the professor's need for students: "You need two more art courses, and you're also deficient in history, so you need one more history course." The peril in all of this is that average people have lost the ability to define their own needs. They have relinquished that responsibility to the professionals. The professional's definition and manufacture of need is guided by their vested economic interests and their own cultural values. The irony is that the need-meeters must create needs in others because their own professional systems are so needy. Clients need courage to doubt the "experts" and faith to believe in their own intuitive sense of need. The professionals, on the other hand, must question their own learned definitions of need and must refrain from participating in the manufacture of artificial need among vulnerable clients.

Makers of Mystery

Another peril in the land of professionalism is the tendency toward mystification. The practice of a profession takes on a mysterious character. Clients find themselves in a strange and unfamiliar land where a foreign language is spoken. The patient on the dentist's chair has no idea of the condition of his teeth as the dentist describes each tooth to the dental assistant in a special jargon that only the dentist and her assistant understand. The client's problem, diagnosis, and prescribed treatment are all encoded in a technical, foreign language which must be translated back into English if the patient is to grasp the nature of the illness and cure. The machinery and sophisticated hardware, the labels for various types of clients, and the treatment philosophies all give a profession a mysterious character.

Braces become "appliances," heart attacks become "myocardial infarctions," doing different jobs becomes "structural-functional differentiation," being naughty is a "behavioral maladjustment." This process of mystification, largely cultivated through the use of special vocabulary, has a number of consequences for the professional-client relationship. First of all, it gives the professional setting and activity an unusual sense of importance. These activities are not ordinary mundane ones like mowing grass, brushing teeth, and driving cars. These professional routines have a special status and prestige. They are more than just everyday maneuvers. Second, the mysterious language permits teams of professionals, for example, doctors and nurses, professors and teaching assistants, psychologists and psychiatric aides to exchange the secrets of the trade without the patient's knowledge. The client or patient wants to know, "Am I really sick?" "Am I really going to die?" "Am I really emotionally disturbed?" "Am I really ignorant?" The client suddenly realizes that the urgent questions and affairs of his own life are being decided and acted upon in his presence by a team of professionals using another language. He is prevented from fully knowing and grasping all aspects of his "problem."

The mysterious vocabulary provides a convenient means of withholding important and relevant information from the client and controlling the "case's" access to the secrets of his case. Unless he has command of the trade language, the client loses control of his situation. The unfamiliarity and awkwardness of the new vocabulary makes it difficult to ask for information. It may be difficult to pronounce the big words, and so one may not even try. Since it is difficult to ask a question with the big words and since it almost seems irreverent or embarrassing to ask a question in everyday words, more often than not the patient or student may simply not ask. Out of the fear of the strange language, the client is paralyzed and loses control of his own life. The fear of asking, although immobilizing to the client, insulates the professional from many sticky and complicated questions.

Mystification generates distance between the client and professional practitioner and places the professional in a role not unlike a priest. The student is here with his very common and everyday questions or problems. The professional has access to a whole body of special and mysterious knowledge beyond the grasp of the patient. The professional mediates between the client and the wisdom accumulated by his profession over time. The professional, as priest, prescribes the remedies and offers hope and salvation for the problem, whether it be anxiety or ignorance. In this sense, the professional bridges the gulf that separates the layperson from the mysterious knowledge of the profession. Although the professional spans this chasm and links the layperson with solutions, this fact also reminds the person of the real distance between himself and the professional. In terms of their knowledge, they are living in two different worlds.

Decoding Mystery

The development of a special language is a typical and natural process, inherent and necessary in a special field of study. The peril of mystification is that the professional may deliberately or unwittingly use the argot to increase the sense of mystery, to limit authentic communication with the client, to cover up professional ignorance by giving the appearance of competence, and to legitimate the prestige of the profession. As with all mystery, there is fear and awe. Fear makes the layman afraid to challenge or question, and awe cultivates an unwarranted sense of worship and respect for the professional and the profession. All of this heightens the power of the professional over the client; herein lies the tremendous appeal to mystify. Good mystery makers have power—enormous power. And there is within every professional endeavor opportunity to accelerate the mystery, rendering the client or student less capable of understanding and dealing with his own problems.

I have seen some professionals do an outstanding job of demolishing the mystery that surrounds their practice. They described complicated health problems in simple, everyday English. I have seen others, quite enamored with their ability to say the big words, hike the mystery to a ludicrous level. What we need are professionals who can translate from "professionalese" to English. Such translators who are willing to relinquish their secrets and honestly speak the truth in everyday language can be instrumental in giving patients a new sense of understanding and control over their own lives.

CHAPTER TWELVE

Neglecting Wholeness and Humility

By Donald B. Kraybill

Splitting Persons

The peril of fragmentation is inherent in the professionalizing process. Modern societies are characterized by an omnipresent and increasing specialization. Professionals are part of this narrowing drift toward refinement. Specialization intrudes on all professions. Family dentists no longer pull teeth. Professors become experts in one of many subdivisions within an academic field. An attorney may focus his practice in one particular aspect of corporate law. Specialization generates distance and fragmentation. Immersed in the intricate complexities of one small slice of life with its special language, rituals, and procedures, professionals become separated from each other and their clients. In addition to the social distance created by specialization, life is sliced or fractured into a series of separate operations.

An assembly line provides a comic image of this fragmentation. Picture individuals riding a conveyor belt which takes them from station to station in the course of a day where experts feed them information or perform an "operation" for them. The weatherman tells them how to dress early in the morning. The news commentator prescribes how the news should be interpreted. The gas station attendant gasses up the car, the waitress delivers breakfast, and on and on through the whole day until the last station where a comedian provides sedative humor on the late night show.

At each station along the line, specialists perform their service for the client. For the most part social relations are cold, calculative, and formal: clients paying for service and specialists providing service for a fee. Most of us both ride the line and operate a station that provides specialized service to others going by. So we are one moment hopping on the line, and the next minute back at our station "serving" others on the line.

The peril of fragmentation has two aspects. Individuals become viewed as a collection of unrelated and specialized problems, for example, "multiproblem cases." Second, the professional is tempted to abdicate responsibility for all other problems except the one for which he is highly trained.

In the first aspect, the individual is sliced up into an assortment of needs, problems, and deficiencies all remedied by separate specialists. There are orthodontists, dentists and oral surgeons for teeth; specialists for feet, ears, hearts, nerves, and brain; experts in marital counseling, child rearing, legal advice, and retirement counseling. The individual's body is literally mapped into problem areas with a super technician and all his gadgets for each problematic region.

The life cycle is similarly compartmentalized. There are, we are told, seven crises in life and four stages in death—or is it five? Already there are experts who specialize as counselors in each of the traumatic crises of life. And probably by the time I'm ready to die there will be five professionally trained counselors, each with a special expertise, to help me cope with each stage of my death.

Not only is the body and life cycle split into separate problem areas, but so are social and emotional relationships. There are divorce attorneys, psychiatrists who counsel children whose parents are separating, sex therapists and school psychologists with special treatments for adolescent learning problems. In addition to the specialists, there are faddish "treatment modalities," "interventions," and "therapies" all designed to zero in on special problems.

It is useful and often comforting to be surrounded by such a host of specialists all geared up to diagnose and treat any sort of predicament, *but* there is also a dehumanizing terror in all of this. There is the possibility that the specialist only cares about correcting the one cog in my machine that's not working and doesn't really care about me as a person.

From the professional's vantage point, there is the strong tendency to deal with an isolated part of an individual's life or body, while forgetting or avoiding the whole. The press of time the specialized training, and myopia of vision together generate the assembly line syndrome of "what's the problem? . . . here's the remedy . . . who's next?"

The assembly line structure of modern professional life is dehumanizing to both client and professional; the client becomes an assortment of broken cogs and the professional provider becomes a technician who is only good at fixing a certain type of cog. Thus, the holistic humanity of both client and provider shrinks to a series of technical routines. There are pleasant exchanges about weather and families during the technological "fix," but often little genuine caring and human sharing. The epitome of this technical compartmentalization is symbolized in two recent operations in separate hospitals where surgeons operated on the wrong patients. In both instances neither surgeon nor patient was aware of the error during the operation. The patient was anesthetized before the surgeon arrived. The surgeon had either not seen the patient before, or didn't recognize the body. And so the wrong problem on the wrong body was fixed without the professional or client recognizing the error.

Outside My Expertise

A second peril of fragmentation is the tendency on the part of the professional to shuck off any sense of responsibility for any other aspect of a client's life than the specific problem within the professional's "area of expertise." While it is true that some professionals can do considerable damage by wandering too far outside their area of competence, the greater damage is in withdrawing into a narrowly confined stance that feels no responsibility and shows no concern for the other aspects of a client's life.

Recently, while teaching a course on complex organizations, I discovered a student in the class who was a recent immigrant

---

Keeping Professions in Their Place

By John A. Lapp

I am a historian (by training), a teacher (for years my means of a livelihood), an administrator (the title I now carry), a churchman (teaching in and administering a church-sponsored institution), a writer (a major source of identity for people who do not know me institutionally). Each of these is a profession. I am a partial professional in each.

One way I keep from being consumed by professionalism is to emphasize this plurality of worlds. The danger is that I become a dilettante, the very opposite of the professional, at least in the sense of expertise.

My own conviction is that the Christian calling can be fulfilled as a professional. But the calling takes precedence. My profession is an instrument. Otherwise I would not know what it means to confess that God is Lord.

---

from South America. She had serious problems reading and writing English. When I talked with her about the deficiencies, I suggested she check with the people in the "writing lab" to see if they could help. I also proposed hiring a special reading tutor, or asking someone in the counseling center to provide special assistance. I urged her to meet weekly with another student taking the same course. In my eagerness to find her special assistance, it never occurred to me that I could work with her to improve her English. After all, I was not trained for such mediocre tasks. I was a specialist; I was here to teach her about the complications of complex organizations. There were other specialists around to help her in these more mundane areas. This was not my problem. Why did the school ever admit someone that couldn't read and write?

Such reasoning is typical of the denial of responsibility that accompanies fragmentation. Professionals, while implying that they don't want to step outside their arena because their incompetence might create injury, can effectively use the slogan "Outside my area of expertise" as a socially polite way to limit their responsibility or involvement with a client.

Professionals tend to think of their clients as a bundle of isolated problems in need of a technological fix. An individual's deficiency is treated as an isolated problem unrelated to other problems, to a social context, and, most importantly, to a real person. Consequently, the professional feels little obligation to the client's whole person and politely remains within the restricting and safe confines of "my area of expertise." Perhaps we need generalized helpers who can provide rudimentary assistance in many areas. In any case, we need professionals who laugh, joke, play, and eat with their clients, and who aren't afraid to step outside of their areas of expertise.

Cultivating Conceit

Professions have many uncanny ways of breeding conceit. In the well-intentioned effort to discover solutions to human problems, answers easily assume an air of arrogance The practicing professional often gives the impression that the latest fads in clinical practice are the final answers to the predicament of the human condition. "Well, there's a new psychotherapy that's designed for precisely this kind of thing." "We have a novel courtroom technique that will persuade any jury." "We've just discovered a new drug that does wonders on this." "Psychologically we know that's how people work." There is a tendency to take the present state of knowledge too seriously, to give the impression, although we know better, that it represents the final word. We may not understand the long-term side effects of a new drug or therapy. It's hard to admit that we really do not know very much about the relative influence of genetic and cultural factors in personality formation. It is easy to overlook the fact that our facts today may be overturned tomorrow. In spite of these limitations with our professional knowledge, there is a propensity to give the impression that we *are* in control of the human condition and that we *do* have definitive answers.

Although it is quite disheartening, it is nonetheless refreshing to hear mature and humble professionals openly admit that they do not know much about certain questions or that what they do know is shaky and likely to be overturned by new research. Professionals can admit the limits of their knowledge to each other, but there is an uncanny pressure in the presence of clients and the general public to at least give the impression that they are on top of things and that their knowledge is adequate. No one likes to pay a professional just to be told that "we're really uncertain about what is the best treatment for that." Professionals who speak the truth in humility may run the risk of sounding quite unprofessional and even incompetent with their answers of "we're unsure about that now."

Each profession cultivates a sense of pride in its members about the unique importance of their work in contrast to rival professions. The police are taught that they have to make the tough "life and death" decisions on the street; they can't enjoy the leisure of an attorney who can consult his library before making a decision. In contrast to the "myopic" view of psychiatrists, social workers believe that they understand individuals in the context of their social systems. Sociologists aren't involved in "mushy caring" like social workers, but think of themselves as objective social scientists unraveling the secrets of human interaction. Economists take a broad liberal arts approach to economic life, careful to avoid the nuts and bolts mentality of the "accountant types." And on and on it goes, with each profession in its own way telling itself, teaching its members, and unfortunately often believing, that its particular emphasis and vantage point embodies the truth in a fuller way than other professions.

Conceit also arises in paternalistic attitudes toward clients. Back-stage jokes among professionals about their students or clients ("You'll never believe what this guy said this morning") betray professional arrogance. "Students are stupid, getting dumber each year, and really don't want to learn." "Patients don't care about their health, don't know what's good for them, and can't even say the name of their disease." A lawyer's clients "have no idea what's going on" and "don't even know where to sign their name."

Implied is an arrogant attitude on the part of the professional that "I know what's good for you and you don't." Such a mind-set makes it difficult for the professor or clinician to really hear the student or client. There may be a polite ritual of "listening," but it can never be authentic listening as long as the professional assumes that the client really doesn't know anything anyway. Beyond the difficulty that professional conceit creates for hearing people is the larger question of evaluation and review.

Professional Isolation

One of the cherished values of professionalism is professional autonomy—a profession should seek as much as possible to free itself of restrictions imposed by others over the conduct of its work. Basic to this is the notion of self-regulation and evaluation. Due to the proficiency of their political organization, their ability to mystify others, and the strength of their vested economic interests, professions have been able to insulate themselves from external review by clients and the general public by perpetuating the myth that laypeople are simply incompetent to evaluate their work. I was recently amazed at the vitality of this myth among professors contemplating student evaluation. The myth of the incompetent layperson took many forms: "How can students evaluate a professor's competence if they don't know anything about the field of study?" "They won't recognize their truly noble teachers until five years later." "They only judge the professor's entertaining ability—not his substance." While all of these facts may be partly true, they are all based on the belief that students are so stupid they can't tell the difference between a good teacher and a poor one. More accurately, resistance to student evaluations is based on the fear that some professors might learn some unpleasant things about their own ineffectiveness that would require change.

The arrogant assumptions that patients don't know when they've been cured, that they can't compare the effectiveness of various treatment procedures, and that they aren't really competent to judge the performance of a profession or its technicians are all constructed by professions to protect their own self-interests. Such myths insulate professions from change and the critique of their clientele. Review and evaluation by peers within the profession who hold similar values, common attitudes, and a vested economic self-interest will not quickly alter a profession's responsiveness to real needs and it severely limits the effectiveness of its service.

Freidson says (1970:370), "A profession quite naturally forms a perspective of its own, a perspective all the more distorted and narrow by its source in a status answerable to no one but itself. Once a profession forms such a self-sustaining perspective, protected from others' perspectives, insulated from the necessity of justifying itself to outsiders, it cannot be expected to see itself and its mission with clear eyes nor can it be reasonably expected to assume the perspective of its clientele. If it cannot assume the perspective of its clientele, how can it pretend to serve it well? Its very autonomy has led to insularity and a mistaken arrogance about its mission in the world. . . . Their (professions') autonomy has created their narrow perspective and their self-deceiving views of themselves and their work, their conviction that they know best what humanity needs. It is time that their autonomy be tempered."

CHAPTER THIRTEEN

Understanding Professional Distance

By Myron Ebersole

> *The great danger of the increasing professionalization of the different forms of healing is that they become ways of exercising power instead of offering service.*
>
> —Henri J. M. Nouwen

The Dilemma of Distance and Intimacy

For the Christian community, concerned with being open, caring, and equal, in interpersonal relationships the power and detachment of the professional is a peculiar problem. The professional person whose identity is shaped by the disciplines and training of his vocation is a threat to the values of the servant community.

The relation between the professional and the non-professional may be characterized by the ambiguities of distance and intimacy, fear and trust, power and dependency, respect and resentment, interdependence and exclusivism, and hopeful antici-pation and anxious dread. One sees both fear and expectation on the faces and people in the waiting rooms of professional helpers. Yet we admit the helping professionals, who hold life-changing knowledge and mysterious power, into the most intimate recesses of our lives.

On the other hand, professional distance is the detachment and objectivity with which the professional person views clients or patients. This quality of detachment is symbolized in the boundary markers between professional and nonprofessional:

academic degrees, titles, certification procedures, licensing, codes of ethics, uniforms and other evidences of entitlement. The power implied by these symbols raises several questions. Will the power be used for the benefit of those served or to enhance the prestige of the professional person? Do these symbols represent the professional person's qualifications and abilities to care for people or do they preserve a sterile noninvolvement? Do these marks of professionalism enable the professional to identify with the needs of persons or are they the marks of professional class distinction? Are these symbols bridges or walls between the professional and client?

"Profession" originally meant the act of professing or taking the vows of a religious order. The Oxford Shorter Dictionary says that by 1675 the word was secularized to mean "that [which] professes to be duly qualified; professional." The qualifying characteristics of professional specialization include: (1) mastery of a body of intellectual *knowledge and theory* and (2) development of *techniques or skills* directed toward (3) *specialized service* in society in return for (4) *set remuneration.* Professionals have developed (5) *professional associations* for the maintenance and development of (6) *responsible standards* governing their practice. Martin Pernick, in an article on "Medical Professionalism" in the *Encyclopedia of Bioethics,* describes the historical development of a "social contract" in which professional groups agree to provide services, prevent abuses, and maintain standards while society agrees to grant them power, freedom, and status.

Professionals live with conflicting demands. They are expected to approach complex problems with cool-headed, unemotional detachment, yet at the same time show empathic understanding and concern for the person(s) being served. They are expected to maintain a balance between the needs of the individuals they serve and the interests of the larger society. They are supposed to perform specialized technical tasks (surgery, writing a legal brief, leading a religious ceremony) with full awareness of the underlying body of generalized knowledge and theory (biology, law and ethics, theology).

"Professionalism" is the composite of attitudes and accepted practices which enable a person to function with optimal effectiveness in a limited field of service. It is difficult to separate that definition from attitudes of exclusivism. However, the purpose of professionalism is not to create a permanent set of values or standards, but to provide a flexible set of guidelines to help resolve and mediate conflicts which arise in interaction with those being served. Thus, Pernick says: "While professional standards help physicians resolve the conflict between empathy and detachment, there is no single universally valid formula that spells out the correct professional mix of concern and distance." Professionalism, therefore, must be an evolving set of solutions for a changing set of problems. Professionalism becomes a problem when it becomes a set of permanently fixed traditional solutions unaffected by the changing needs of the human community.

The Christian professional recognizes the tension between the call of professionalism and his commitments to the kingdom of God. But it is too simple to reject professionalism. We must examine professional practice and modify its relational style with a primary commitment to serve in the spirit of Christ. In this light, professional distance is an acceptable form of relationship only if it in some way facilitates superior care and service to the person who comes for help.

The Necessity of Distance

Objectivity has long been valued as a prerequisite to sound professional judgment. Because objectivity demands an element of emotional detachment, physicians do not treat members of their own famililes. The lawyer who defends himself in court is said to have a "fool for a client." In the psychotherapeutic professions, there are extensive efforts in the development of self-understanding by the therapist—in the supervision of their training and in the use of consultants—to achieve a level of "objectivity about one's own subjectivity." This is aimed at moving the therapeutic process forward without entangling the therapist's feelings. Further, the patient requires some social distance for the freedom "to be myself" without the disruptive intensity of emotions elicited by a therapist who "knows me inside and out." This is the other side of intimacy: creating a setting where the patient feels safe enough to reveal the secrets of the inner self. These secrets have been called "guilty knowledge" by Everett Hughes. While revealing the guilty knowledge to the professional may not alter the reality of the guilt, the guilty one is afforded a safe place to explore the implications of the hidden and learn how to handle it responsibly. The "objective" professional distance creates a private place of refuge which is often impossible among intimate social friends.

Within any relationship, effective helping requires some degree of objective distance. The level of objectivity varies from one type of interaction to another. A physician undoubtedly requires more objectivity than a parent in relation to the child. However, even in the primary relationships of the family and in the close-knit fellowship of the church, the valued objectivity of a wiser person and, in some instances, of a noninvolved third person is needed to resolve conflict. Jesus' instructions on conflict resolution in Matthew 18 illustrate this point.

Finally, distance or objectivity in helping relationships does not mean indifference. The ability to be a helping resource, while calling for objective judgment undistorted by emotions, does require intentional attentiveness to the person receiving help. Renee Fox in her *Experiment Perilous* called this kind of objectivity "detached concern." It may be in reality a form or discipline of helping. However, when distance becomes a way of avoiding interpersonal involvement in an excluding or self-protective manner, the role of intimacy must be established as the other dimension of the helping relationship.

The Necessity of Intimacy

Dr. Karl Menninger, the widely known leader of the Menninger Clinic in Topeka, Kansas, told a group of psychiatric residents that the most important part of the therapeutic process is "diagnosis." He meant that accurate diagnosis is the basis of all effective treatment. It might seem that he is describing another aspect of objective distancing. However, he approached diagnosis as a constant process of being in touch with the inner-life experience of the patient. He also defined psychotherapy as the "constant refinement of hypotheses" about the meaning of patients' thoughts, feelings, behavior, and experience. Henri Nouwen says the word diagnosis means "to know through and through."

Professional helpers who are known for their effectiveness recognize that intense interpersonal relations conflict with the distance and coolness of objective observation in the therapeutic process. However, they also know that adequate understanding occurs only when there is a common task of exploration, and only when the objective viewpoint is suspended to allow the helper to experience empathetically the inner life of the other. Thus both distance and nearness are required for effective client-professional relationships. The professional must deal with the instabilities that result when it is necessary to overcome distance to achieve inner knowledge or intimacy. At the same time the helper must be willing to interrupt subjective identification with the client in order to achieve a clearer objective viewpoint. The effective professional helper must maintain a delicate balance between distance and intimacy. This process of "knowing-diagnosis" is more than a technique. It cannot be applied as a mechanical skill. It requires the full investment of self in the art of active listening and in being present to the other person. Martin Buber described it as the "powerful moment of dialogic" where "deep calls into deep." For Nouwen the healing function is found in the use of biblical hospitality that enables the "stranger" to understand his own needs. He says, "Healing is the humble but very demanding task of creating and offering a friendly empty space where strangers can reflect on their pain and suffering without fear and find the confidence that makes them look for new ways right in the center of their confusion." While this may sound like a description of a supportive church fellowship, it is equally important in the healing activity of the professional helper when the person's needs require specialized help.

Intimacy gives dynamic balance and enriches the positive meaning of distance. The more technical concept of empathy can serve as another focus for the study of this issue.

Toward a Covenant Model

I have suggested that a balance between distance and intimacy resolves the dilemma in the professional's attitudes toward those he or she serves. For the Christian there remains the deeper question of the professional's self-understanding in helping relationships. I would like to suggest the biblical concept of *covenant* as a transcendent model for professional relations. Before describing the covenant model, I will identify three other commonly used models as outlined by William May, (1975).

Philanthropy is a common professional model sometimes used self-consciously to reinforce the service motive. It involves the role of a superior giving aid to an inferior with a quality of spontaneous generosity, but it in fact denies the reality of the professional exchange. Its tendency to demean the recipient actually increases distance.

Code relationships are determined by rules, habits, and accepted practice. The code, both as prescribed by the professional association and by generally accepted practice, is one way in which the profession lives up to its end of the social contract with the general public. Personal interests take secondary place while professional standards determine the nature of the professionals' relations. From the Christian perspective it entails all the dangers of demonic professionalism mentioned earlier. This model requires little compassion or "suffering with" the client.

The *contract* serves to effectively delineate the terms of professional-client relationships. Relationships are defined in legally enforceable terms including rights, duties, qualifications, and conditions. The client, together with the professional, sets the terms of the agreement, though in actual practice the professional has primary control. Its limitation from the Christian perspective is the absence of giving oneself in the human relationships since the exchange is determined on a barter basis.

In contrast, the *covenant* model has relational, historical, and promissory connotations. The common elements of all covenants include an original gift, a promise based on the original gift, an anticipated exchange, mutual respect, loyalty, and giving behavior by the participants in the promises of the covenant. The biblical setting of the covenant meal in the context of hospitality adds to the richness of this understanding.

In the context of professional relationships, the covenant elements include: (1) the gift of society's investment in the training and development of the professional technology and skills, and then the opportunity to practice given to the professional by his clients. (2) The client reciprocates through paying fees, but even more deeply by sharing the gratification of professional accomplishment, and the agreement to participate in the dynamic therapeutic process in which both participants learn and grow. (3) The covenant model for the professional-client relationship is characterized by respect and caring, the depths of which is limited only by the limitations of time, energy, and appropriateness.

May (1975) related the covenant model specifically to its religious roots:

> The indebtedness of a human being that makes his life—however sacrificial—inescapably responsive cannot be fully appreciated by totaling up the varying sacrifices and investments made by others in his favor. Such sacrifices are there; and it is lacking in honesty not to acknowledge them. But the sense that one is inexhaustibly the object of a gift presupposes a more transcendent source of donative activity than the sum of gifts received from others. For the biblical tradition this transcendent was the secret root of every gift between human beings, of which the human order of giving and receiving could only be a sign. Thus the Jewish Scriptures enjoin: When you harvest your crops, do not pick your fields too clean.... Their ethic of service to the needy flowed from Israel's original and continuing state of neediness and indebtedness before God. Thus action which at a human level appears gratuitous, in that it is not provoked by a specific gratuity from another human being, is at its deepest level but gift answering to a gift. This responsivity is theologically expressed in

the New Testament as follows: "In this is love, not that we loved God but that he loved us . . . if God so loved us, we also ought to love one another" (1 John 4:10-11).

It is possible to be a professional and a Christian. The ambiguities of professional distance, power, and intimacy are subject to creative resolution. This can occur when the individual professional (and hopefully the professional society) recognizes that the essence of human life is found in living relations and that those relations are based on the original transcendant gift. When professional relations are thought about in this way, professional distance, instead of being authority over the client, will be bridged by the commitment to be a servant. In this context the professional person will find it possible to break through the barriers created by self-serving professionalism to create a new community of caring.

CHAPTER FOURTEEN

Setting Fees

By Wallace and Evelyn Shellenberger

Behind the Charge

Setting a charge for services provided is not a simple problem for the Christian professional. Ideally, a charge benefits both client and professional. The professional agrees to perform a certain service for a stated price which the client will pay unless negotiated otherwise. The charge formalizes that agreement and both parties' responsibilities. For example, when parents are facing a significant discipline problem the charge may help to put that concern in perspective. Is my child's behavior problem serious enough that I would be willing to pay $15.00 or $30.00 to discuss it with a professional counselor? Will the money be well spent? The structure of a charge provides a counterbalance to a more subjective perception of need.

The professional, knowing that his or her service will be paid for, is freed, at least in part, from the potential negative feelings of being used or taken advantage of. This may increase the quality of service provided. For example, when a doctor is called out of bed at 2:00 a.m. to sew up a person who was cut in a drunken brawl, knowing that the service will be paid for makes it easier to care for that person. For both the client and the professional, the charge clarifies the contract and helps to put potential feelings into perspective.

The Clients' View

Client wants accessible service. They are concerned with the impact of the charge on their finances. Usually the more accessible the service, the higher the charge. The size of professionals' fees signals the kind and type of population they wish to serve. The fees of psychiatrists in private practice may make their services unavailable to some persons in need of counseling.

Some needs are more acute than others. The more needed the service, the more a client is willing to pay. A mother will pay an emergency room fee of $30.00 for the care of a child with a sprained ankle but may not pay $15.00 for a well child's examination and immunizations. It is easier to pay a dentist $100.00 to repair a decayed tooth that has pained you all night than to shell out $20.00 for a routine dental check when you are feeling fine.

Clients sometimes judge the worth or value of a service by the cost. This may be particularly true with those who purchase professional service hoping to benefit from a magical power. But, "you get what you pay for" does not necessarily apply to professional service as it does to merchandise. There are instances when clients have no other way of evaluating the quality of professional service except by comparing cost.

The size of the charge is not, however, a reliable measure of the quality of the service. A nurse practitioner may charge $10.00 to do a physical examination on an infant whereas a pediatrician may charge $15.00 for doing the same service. Clients may assume that the pediatrician does a more thorough evaluation of the child. In reality, the quality of the examination may be identical and the nurses' care might be superior.

A psychiatrist in a community mental health center saw a client who questioned the value of his service because of the comparatively low fee. In further conversations the client acknowledged that until his recent financial ruin, he dealt with large sums of money and anchored his personal identity on having "two grand in my pocket." High quality service to him meant paying high prices regardless of the quality of the service.

We were surprised some time ago by the realism of our

patients. We had struggled for months about whether or not to raise our office visit charge. We finally decided to increase the charge and braced ourselves for the reaction. To our surprise there was none. Their accepting response was, "We've been expecting it; everything else is going up."

A Christmas Wish

By Lawrence S. Eby

One of the dilemmas I face in private medical practice is how to set and collect fees. I have always wanted to give service irrespective of a client's ability to pay. Physicians have traditionally seen patients without requiring payment at the time the service is rendered, and also have not charged interest for unpaid balances. It is difficult, however, to identify those people who really cannot afford medical care. In a sense, anyone with large medical bills feels they cannot afford to pay if they do not have some form of insurance. Yet many people have chosen to go without insurance, gambling that they would not have large medical bills.

In December one of my office employees reported that there was a family with an unpaid account who she felt had real financial difficulties. She offered to contribute her usual Christmas bonus toward the cancellation of the debt. This stimulated me to think about the many unpaid accounts which had accumulated over three and a half years, some small, some large. I decided to cancel those which were more than one to two years old with a Christmas wish for a happy holiday season. The exact wording was:

> It has now been many months since I was of some service to you as a physician. I presume you have not paid due to financial hardship on your part. I hope the canceling of this bill will make your Christmas more joyous.
> P.S. If your financial status improves, share it with a needy person.

In the next week or two a few of these people sent or brought in either partial or total payment of the unpaid accounts. From the others I heard nothing. But it relieved me from worrying about what to do with these accounts without getting involved in some kind of coercive litigation.

I personally felt good about this experience, but don't hold it up as an ideal way of dealing with every situation. Fortunately, most of my patients do pay. A professional in a different situation, with a large percentage of unpaid accounts, may need a sterner approach.

Some clients find certain charges genuinely oppressive. These may be the "good patients" or "good clients." They realize they need services; they agree to purchase them; they follow the recommendations, but indebt themselves for years to meet the expenses. Clients who are not covered by government or private insurance feel particularly oppressed when they see the professionals who "serve" them receiving an income three or four times greater than their own.

Most clients appreciate openness about charges and welcome an opportunity to discuss them with the professional. The charge is an important vehicle in the client-professional relationship. The professional takes and the client gives. But there are also times when the professional should give and the client should take in establishing fees. Done in a spirit of openness, such a discussion usually strengthens the relationship. Without this openness, the client may not pay, or may pay resentfully; or the professional may reluctantly write off an uncollectable account. In either case the relationship is injured. Openness is mutually beneficial.

The Professional's View

Professionals, like everyone else, are concerned about self-worth, power, and success. Power and self-worth are closely linked with being able to request and receive a charge for services. Being able to set high fees and receive a good income entices people to believe they are truly great and successful.

Most professionals charge what others do who are in the same discipline. Often the first question asked is, "What is the going rate?" "What are other psychologists, lawyers, etc., charging?" When this happens, the Christian professional may be uncritically perpetuating a fee structure which is oppressive and based on dubious ethical assumptions.

Insurance coverage for charges in the medical and counseling fields has a subtle but definite impact on fee setting. Part of the professional charge for service provides income for the professional. Therefore, issues relating to professional income, salary, benefits, and lifestyle have a direct bearing on the amount of the charge. Our society rewards individual advancement rather than communal achievement. So professionals are nudged to competitively seek individual advancement. One's desired income and lifestyle may significantly determine the set charges.

It is costly to fuel a "professional" lifestyle necessary to maintain a "professional" image among "professional" peers, if one so desires. A certain type of house, car, vacation, clothing, club membership, and hobby must be maintained. These necessitate a high income which "justifies" high fees for service; the high fees can't be too bad since "they're not out of line with our professional peers."

The professional who chooses to follow in the way of Jesus will be tortured with many questions: What is the reference point from which I determine my lifestyle and income? How much should I be influenced by how my professional peers and the general public think a lawyer, college professor, or physician

---

Not Professional Enough

By Phil M. Shenk

It was one of those times I'd rather forget.

She was an enterprising free-lance reporter out trying to make contacts and get assignments.

I was the yet-damp-behind-the-ears news editor for *Sojourners,* a monthly Christian magazine.

She had introduced herself with skill, sending tear sheets of her work as a big city journalist, an outline of her upcoming Africa travel plans, and a clear sense of why and what she wanted to write for us.

By the time we sat down to talk, I was rather excited. Often our contributors aren't professional writers, but activists or scholars who write for us at night or on weekends during their off-hours. Their copy usually needs much editorial attention. Here was the promise of flawless, incisive news writing.

We spent a half-hour going over possible story ideas, and came up with an exciting handful. Suddenly, just as she began to ask, I realized something else had to be discussed. Money.

"By the way," I blurted out, "we don't pay for articles."

It was as if I had impugned her

should live? How do I deal with the issues of professional success and self-worth in my own life? How much more money should I receive with eight years of post-college training than other professionals with only four years? How much more should I make per hour of work than my receptionist? What community am I using as a reference point in my decision making?

The Biblical View

As Jesus demonstrated God's love through his life and teachings, he served the poor, the captives, the blind, and the oppressed. Being his followers, we have a mandate to love as he loved. That means expecting nothing in return. Jesus speaks of our heavenly Father whose good gifts are not dependent on a reciprocal relationship. What does this mean about the reciprocal relationship implied in the professional-client contract? Is there a suggestion here that the service to one in need should be pro-

---

mother. She took it badly.

It is tough enough to survive as a free-lance writer, especially when you are out on the road. But it's the kiss of death not to be paid.

I felt compelled to break the silence by explaining to her our policy—we're a low-budget ministry to which many people, including our writers, donate time and money.

It was awkward. I could see all the familiar arguments welling up, points that the church has long elicited from artists of all sorts. Why do you pay janitors and printers but not musicians,

dramatists, or writers?

Only her body language asked these questions. Verbally, we both just stumbled around for a short while. Then she left.

As the handful of exciting story ideas slipped like sand through my hand, I realized the more we look like a professional magazine, the more awkward it gets explaining our unique differences. She was surprised by how different we were from the company we keep, how unprofessionally professional we were. It's a nice secret to keep when you can. It's embarrassing when you can't.

vided regardless of the charge to be levied? Jesus goes on to ask, "For if you love those who love you, what reward have you?"

Jesus' words have at least two implications in setting charges for services. First, we must take care that we do not further oppress those we serve and that we do not limit access to service for the poor through our charge for service. Second, we are to love and serve not for others' sake but for Christ's sake, not for what we can expect from others but because God loves us and enables us to love.

Jesus also speaks to the issue of greatness and success. Although success is measured in our society by financial status, Jesus makes it clear that to succeed in his way may mean to fail in the world's eye; to be great, one may appear to be lowly. Jesus, our example, "emptied himself, taking the form of a servant."

Several months ago we were struggling with unpaid accounts. We were trying to decide how to deal with persons and families for whom we provide medical services but who would not pay, even though they probably could. We decided to use a personal approach instead of the legal system in seeking payment. Some clients told us that we were naive to use personal collection methods and that we would continue to be "taken advantage of" if we did. We began to realize how foolish and stupid we appeared to our medical peers and others in the community as we kept on providing services under such circumstances.

From where do we take our cues? Is our reference point our image in the professional and economic community, or is it faithfulness to the example of Jesus?

Setting the Charge

In professional practice, a standard charge is generally set and everyone is expected to pay it. Sometimes the expert may personally set the charge for each service, based on his knowledge of the client's finances and the cost of the service performed.

Another practice is to apply a formula to each client, based on his or her ability to pay. For example, someone with an income of $20,000.00 might pay $20.00 and a client with an income of $10,000.00 might pay $10.00. This system of sliding fees has many problems and is difficult to administer. However, it makes service more available to everyone regardless of income.

We find that a set charge, coupled with a formula for discounting when the need arises, has worked best. Our administrator has developed a discount formula linked with an incentive to pay. For example, if a patient is eligible by a financial assessment to receive a 50 percent discount, we discount an additional dollar every time the patient pays one dollar on the bill.

We have repeatedly found that whether the discount is determined by formula or by the judgment of the expert, it is important that the professional discuss it with the client. A client's self-esteem suffers if he or she is told of a discount by the receptionist on the way out, but it is bolstered if discussed with the professional in the context of their relationship.

What or who will make up the difference when a charge is discounted? The professional may accept a smaller net income. If the professional works on a salary, income from the clients who do pay may offset the discounts given. In our medical practice many paying clients are annoyed when they learn that their payments help support the cost of care for others who will not or cannot pay. On such occasions we try to be sensitive to their concern but also help them understand and accept a broader definition of social responsibility. Regardless of the method, the Christian professional must have some way of discounting charges for those who need service but cannot pay.

Collecting the Charge

When a service is rendered it is expected that the fee will be paid. A contract has been agreed upon between the professional and client. But what if that contract is broken by the client and, for some reason, valid or not, the fee is not paid? What approach should be taken?

Small claims court, credit bureaus, collection agencies, and the local prosecuting attorney can all be hired to make collections. Should the Christian professional use such agencies to collect charges? Are the collection methods consistent with a Christian approach of love and kindness? Are there better means to collect unpaid fees? Does avoiding collection cultivate and perpetuate irresponsibility?

Whenever possible the collection problems should be addressed directly between professional and client and not be delegated to other personnel. Clients prefer to deal directly with the professional in these problems.

In our practice we emphasize the importance of carefully reviewing each individual case when fee collection has failed. By doing this we sort out those who cannot pay from those who will not pay, continue to be personally involved in the collection process, and insure that noncoercive methods are used. We have decided to use the small claims court as the last resort in collecting from those persons who could pay but wouldn't. We feel this decision takes the above objectives into consideration, yet requires accountability of patients with the ability to pay.

Some Guidelines for Consideration

In summary, the professional who takes seriously the life and teaching of Jesus must give serious consideration to the implications of setting fees for service. The following guidelines warrant serious attention in the process of deciding the size, administration, and collection of charges.

1. The charges should not be oppressive.
2. One's professional lifestyle should be intentional rather than imitative of other professionals.
3. One's professional salary should be related to genuine financial need, with the church as the reference point rather than the professional group.
4. Differentials in salaries among occupations within the church should be minimal.
5. Charges should not prohibit access to service by those who need it.
6. Personal, noncoercive means should be used in the collection of fees.
7. There should be discussion and accountability between the professional and the church in carrying out these guidelines.

CHAPTER FIFTEEN

Playing Monopoly

By Howard Raid

Apples and Diamonds

The sessions that seem to get the most attention at conventions for professionals are the ones on "How to Become More Professional." To be called a professional provides one with instant status in our society. To be accused of acting unprofessional is a criticism.

In the past, the professions have included medicine, pastoral ministry, teaching, law and other similar occupations. Recently, however, the definition has expanded to include many other occupations which provide a service but usually not a product. All of these "professions" are supposed to serve people directly. They have, however, the usual human temptation to become self-serving, often by developing a monopoly.

Most of us have rather strong feelings about a business organization that has a monopoly, like our local utilities. We feel helpless to do anything about them. But we realize that if we wish to use their product or service, we have to support the monopoly. So our frustrations increase and we eagerly support political action to "control" business monopolies. Teddy Roosevelt became a folk hero because he came riding fearlessly out of the plains of South Dakota to "bust the trusts." Today we rush to join the "consumer movement" in our own attempt to "bust the trusts." Yet in spite of all of our political and public activity, the monopolies continue to grow.

What is the nature of this strange "animal" that "everyone" is against and yet supports? What is a monopoly? Most people think of it as a huge corporation that is so tightly organized that a customer's concern never gets past a computer's response. While a few monopolies may be of this nature, such as the DeBeers' diamond firm, many are small in size. But basically they all have the same quality. They control something of value that cannot be taken away by competition. When Stark Brothers brought the first Delicious apple tree into commercial production, they had a monopoly. There was only one Delicious apple. So if you wanted that kind of apple, you had to buy it from Stark Bros. If you want to buy a diamond anywhere in the world, you probably will pay a price that is set by the worldwide DeBeers' firm. Monopoly is the control of an economic resource that is scarce. This means that there is not enough of that resource for all to have as much as they want, at a price they are able to pay. Furthermore, it means that the control of that resource is in the hands of a single person, firm, or group.

Hoarding Service

Apples and diamonds are examples of product monopoly, but the same idea applies to providing services. If you are a lawyer who is very skilled in winning certain types of cases, you can create a monopoly among lawyers in that field. Soon you will be able to charge your clients almost any amount and they will continue to use your services. Likewise, a medical doctor who is skilled in a certain type of treatment also can develop a monopoly. In each case, the individual controls the amount of service supplied and the price charged.

But consider the other professionals who are not especially skilled. They are weak economically when operating alone and often compete against each other for business. They may attempt to secure a monopoly by organizing a "professional society." This may start innocently when a group of professional friends gets together to talk about common problems. Next they get the idea that "we ought to have a publication to share our insights."

Then they have an annual meeting to report their findings and research. They soon discover that some people are practicing in "their field" who are not "properly educated." Standards must be passed before one can become a "certified" member of the society. If too many begin to join, the standards are raised so that the income of the original members can be maintained and expanded. Gradually a powerful monopoly emerges with a group of people seeking to serve themselves. There are, for all practical purposes, no differences between the so-called "professional association" and the business company. Each is composed of a group of people which is formed basically to serve and protect itself, even though it does offer a product or service that the public wants.

The professional monopoly maintains itself just like any other monopoly. Whenever a new product or service attempts to compete in a controlled trade area, the monopolies seek restrictions to limit that entry.

The same situations occur in all professions. The National Education Association (NEA) is an example of a strong monopoly of "professional people." When it was organized, many public school administrators encouraged their teachers to join. The feeling was that the *NEA Journal* provided helpful teaching aids, as did the annual teacher's meetings. Then the control of the NEA shifted toward those who changed it into a labor union. This is one of the most powerful professional groups in our country. They have members in every voting precinct in our country. They have forced the federal government to establish a Department of Education. An official of the NEA has boasted, "We're the only union with our own cabinet department." At a recent political party convention the NEA had more delegates than any other special interest group. They played an important role in the nomination of the presidential candidate. It is clear that many so-called "professional" groups use the same political tactics as business monopolies.

The professionals are also the new capitalists in our country. Instead of land, buildings, machinery, and materials, the professionals' capital consists of specialized skills. It is often lodged in their ability to use words. Like capitalists, professionals often attempt to make a greater return than their variable or "out of pocket costs." They attempt to get a return on their investment in their capital, their training. They operate like capitalist cabinetmakers who charge more for their products than the cost of material and labor. Professionals do not use the word profit, but the return amounts to the same. And professionals are seldom criticized for their profit.

Likewise, professionals can organize and strengthen their monopoly by the support of the public. Surprisingly, this monopoly is readily accepted by the public. Perhaps part of the reason for this acceptance is the impression that raising the standards for membership automatically insures better service to the public. Because of this, the public is more willing to accept the price increases of a professional group than of a business, perhaps because the word "profit" is not used.

The Grip of Professional Societies

Professional societies require a great deal of their members in order to maintain their monopoly. Members must give their full loyalty to the organization. Most professional societies require certain courses of study, attendance at meetings, and payment of dues. But for professional advancement, the unwritten rules are probably more important. To accommlish this, one meets the important people in the society. Their books and journal articles must be read, at least enough to quote from them. Every effort must be made to make a presentation at the annual conventions. Even the briefest presentation is a "foot in the door," hopefully leading to future opportunities. These presentations must use endless quotes to prove that one has read a great deal of material. The language must be the jargon of the profession, with care to use the fad words of the moment. Adding a bit of statistical analysis or some research done by computer greatly enhances a paper. All of these activities strengthen one's position within the professional monopoly.

The requirements of a professional monopoly were reported in the *Wall Street Journal* of August 19, 1980, in an article about top management people: "Most believe a successful career requires personal sacrifices, and most put their jobs before their families or themselves." The family gets whatever crumbs of time and energy are left over after the race for professional advancement. Furthermore, the family must be very understanding and supportive: "Now run along and watch TV and do not bother (father or mother) until they have completed this very important address they will give to the Society of _____." This sort of loyalty demanded by the profession is undoubtedly one of the reasons so many homes are breaking up in our society. The number of breakups is greatly increased when both the father and mother belong to professional groups that monopolize their time. One of the graduates of Bluffton College told me that in order to advance professionally he had to dress in a certain manner, live in a designated section of town, and associate with selected people. As a result, he changed jobs.

Joining the Monopoly

The professional process begins in the educational system, especially in college. There the future professionals encounter professors who are completely wrapped up in their own discipline. When students find a prof they like, they tend to imitate him, sometimes his mannerisms, but surely his ideas. Often this is the basis for a student's selection of a major field of study. In class, constant reference is made to the "great" people in this particular discipline. Their writings are assigned readings. Their theories and ideas are discussed. If possible, some of these heroes even appear on campus. Such an occasion is a highlight of the school year when the lowly students have the opportunity to personally meet the "great" people of the discipline.

In graduate school the pressure really mounts for budding professionals. The professor spends most of his time in research for pay, consulting for pay, and attending professional meetings. In the classroom he reports about these great experiences.

Students soon find out that even these profs are not very objective or open-minded. Therefore, they must give the professors "right answers" if they want a degree. The professor has often "sold his soul" to the profession. He cannot see any other way of life. Therefore, students find that to get the degree they, too, have to literally "sell their souls" to the profession. Since graduate students have almost been forced to accept the attitude of the professional professor in order to secure their degree, it becomes easy for them to assume that any earlier experience they have had with a "call from God" was mistaken. Such a call is hardly applicable now, after receiving the "great insights" of the profession. Furthermore, how can the "call from God" advance their professional lives?

How can Christians stand up to this tremendous pressure to give themselves completely to a profession? Such resistance is possible only if they are strongly anchored in a faith that they understand, believe, and practice.

Protecting the Monopoly

In our local retirement home, women can no longer wash each other's hair or help one another set it. They are now required to have a licensed hair dresser come to the home to do this complicated service. A highly skilled woodworker with years of experience cannot teach in high school without a certificate, while a completely inexperienced person may teach as long as he or she has a certificate.

While the public believes there may be "secrets" in a profession, most of the monopoly power comes from the structure of the organization. Many of the so-called "secrets" are known to other workers in that field (paramedics, for example, can perform many of the physician's services). Frequently the weakest professionals rush to join the societies to get the protection they offer, while the most skilled can get along without that security. Many people who have been able to secure teaching certificates are incompetent in the classroom. These people are protected by the professional group so that it is difficult to dismiss them.

In the field of accounting one of the highest professional ranks is Certified Public Accountant. Everything that the C.P.A. knows may be learned by any other accountant who is willing to study and work as hard. Yet if that same very capable accountant passes the exam (and they are not very easy) and becomes a C.P.A., his status is greatly advanced. I well remember my first encounter with a C.P.A., about 40 years ago. I was just starting a quarrying business with my brothers in Iowa, and we wanted to bid on a contract with the state of Iowa. We had to have our accounting statements certified, so I took them to a stranger who was a C.P.A. He glanced at the statements, asked a question or two, and signed his name. "That will be $_____." I paid what amounted to half my monthly salary. Yes, I was impressed. That C.P.A. had monopoly power. Whether he was more competent than other accountants, I do not know. All that mattered in that case was that he was a C.P.A. Often in our society we have to use the professional, not necessarily for what they know, but for the position they hold.

Faith Confronts Monopolies

Christians are warned about the "powers that be." Professionalism gives us the illusion of "the way" but in the end it destroys faith because it is self-seeking and self-serving.

The way of the Christian is in sharp contrast to that of the monopoly. The two can never be compatible. A monopoly seeks to withhold its product or service from others until it can get a high price. Christianity shares what it has with those in need without asking what it will get in return. Faithful Christians do not seek to strengthen their monopolistic control over their resources. A monopoly seeks every possible means of restricting competition. It may get laws passed, control credit, or buy up possible substitutes. True Christianity never hides its weakness behind a law or power play, nor forces its acceptance on people.

The Christian has an opportunity as a member of a

professional association to refocus the service dimension of its programs. Said Jesus, "Inasmuch as ye have done it unto one of the least of these my brethren, ye have done it unto me." The truly professional person provides the highest level of service to the weakest member of society as well as to the most powerful. He or she does not seek his or her own gain or "rights" but chooses to serve others.

One professional group makes this pledge, "In all my relations with clients, I agree to observe the following rules of conduct: I shall in the light of all circumstances surrounding my client, make every conscientious effort to ascertain and understand and give that service which, had I been in the same circumstance, I would have applied to myself." In the words of Jesus, "Therefore all things whatsoever ye would that men should do to you, do ye even so to them." Christian professionals use their professional skills in service to others regardless of whether or not they advance their professional status by that service.

CHAPTER SIXTEEN

Whom Shall I Serve?

By Theron F. Schlabach

Power, Institutions, and the Kingdom

Whom shall I, a Christian professional, aim to serve? The obvious answers are so simple they seem naive. Like any follower of Jesus, we are to seek "first the kingdom of God and his righteousness. . . ." As professionals, we serve folks who really need the services.

But sensitive Christian professionals have learned that they face two problems: first, professions in modern society are paths to power which become entangled with ambitions and power patterns that are enemies of kingdom values. Indeed, they are often enemies even of service. Second, professions are interwoven also with complex modern organizations. They are very institutional—because of their histories, and because their techniques often cost so much that only institutions that are alarmingly powerful and complex can marshal the resources to carry them out.

The professions start with confidence in human technique, a confidence that can really become an idolatrous personal faith. Many people, once they have gained professional power and skills, do not seem to be among the "poor in spirit." Therefore some Christians may say that at the heart of professionalism there is enmity toward God. Others of us see the matter as one of keeping professionalism and its power in a proper place—that is, under our commitment that Jesus is Lord and under a devotional approach to God, to his creation, and to life. "Seek ye first the kingdom" invites us to know what is ultimate and what is not. Confidence in human technique, professional codes of etiquette and conduct, and the powers that come with professional skills must be for us far from ultimate.

Professor X and the Big Red Machine

Almost every Christian professional has had moments when professionalism bumped hard against ideals. I got my first real professional knocks as a graduate student in the early 1960s at the University of Wisconsin. The department of history, my professional home there, was producing some fine scholarship but was perhaps too conscious of playing Avis to the Hertzes of the Northeast. Some of our faculty role models acted as if they meant it when they jokingly referred to their profession as a "racket."

Among such professors was Professor X with whom I worked closely. Quick and clever, he was like good theater: his ideas, values, and style always evoked response, positive or negative. He himself had grown up in blue-collar Pittsburgh with a Calvinist piety. One of his aims was to turn parochial students into "smart" professionals. It was almost a Calvinistic calling for him. "Knocking the fuzz off their brains," was his general term for it. An officer of the local chapter of the American Association of University Professors, he also worked to protect faculty professional interests. On at least one occasion he gave lengthy advice to graduate students about how to protect professors' jobs, even when (as he admitted) it might mean foisting an incompetent teacher onto students.

The department ran what graduate students awesomely dubbed its "big red machine," designed to launch new PhD sellers into careers and at the same time build the department's reputation. PhD sellers enjoyed a favorable market in those days, and the machine was efficient. Its design: "You play the professional game and let us tell you where to go, and we'll find

you the best job out there." Advised Professor X, "Don't tell us
you don't want to go to this city or that city because your wife
wants to play in the Little Theater." Or again, equally blithely:
"Don't tell us you won't go to Mississippi, even if they **will** lynch
Negroes on your front porch." The path to success was through
the red machine's maw.

Some of us were skeptical. We skeptics still took comfort
that the machine was there, for at least we did not have to starve
unless we chose to, but we were skeptical. Professor X knew that
Schlabach was skeptical, and for a long time we sparred. Finally,

> X: "Well Theron, shall we nominate you for that job at thus and thus
> university?"
>
> S: "I've kind of expected a job to open at Goshen College [my Men-
> nonite-run alma mater]. If it does, I want to consider it."
>
> X: (Pause: an earnest, evangelical, even kindly expression.) "Theron,
> how can you ever do anything so goddamned stupid? You don't need
> a Wisconsin education to teach at Goshen. You know, in those small
> colleges you'll work harder than in a good university, you'll have all
> the problems, and they'll pay you miserably."
>
> S: "Well, it's a matter of value system."
>
> X: "Value system hasn't a goddamned thing to do with it! It's what you
> get paid!"
>
> S: "You can't really believe that."

I'm not quite sure how the exchange ended. I still doubt that
Professor X really believed fully the version of professionalism he
had accepted. By his own rules, he was a man of integrity. When
no offer came from Goshen College, he helped me put an arm
and a leg into the red machine, nominating me for a position or
two. Then Goshen College sent its offer, and I accepted.

For a time our relationship remained proper; there were no
clever exchanges on values. Meanwhile a close friend of mine
told Professor X, "You must remember those Mennonites have a
strong sense of community." Then one day the professor
telephoned me to say he had read a certain chapter of my
dissertation and wanted to deliver it to our apartment. When he
arrived, he wanted to come in to talk. He said: "You know,
Theron, it's good to know where you're from. Even if you're just

a northern Indiana Mennonite, it's good to know where you're from."

With that mixed signal a warmer friendship resumed. But neither of us had won. I went to Goshen and he continued vigorously to be a professional in his own way.

Answer A: The Christian Institution

My value system answer proceeded from a straightforward formula: Professions like mine function in institutional settings. Institutions revolve around goals and values, and they are much more powerful than the individual. To work for one's own values, then, the sensible course is to align with an institution

---

Why I Preach in the City

By Freeman Miller

When I first decided to come to Philadelphia's inner city as a seminary graduate to take a pastorate at Diamond Street Mennonite Church, I surprised many of my friends and colleagues. Some muttered, "What a waste of education!" "God would have to do a lot of homework to get me into the inner city!" "How can you possibly think of raising a family there?" "How will a seminary education have anything to do with the problems of the inner city?"

The church, along with the business and political community, has too often written off the inner city as irredeemable. We have washed our hands, walked away in disgust, and pronounced the city doomed forever. We find it easier to respond to a call to missionary work in the "dangerous jungles" of the Third World than to respond to a call for working in the complexities of our own urban centers.

There is a large gap between the inner-city cultural milieu and that of suburban or rural America. But we exacerbate those differences by avoiding personal contact. When one decides to live in the midst of an inner-city neighborhood, there are surprising discoveries. One finds a warm and open people often linked together by strong bonds which we have lost in our more affluent neighborhoods. Here are people receptive and eager to work together for improvement. There is a deep kinship in a common struggle against the powers of evil and oppression.

whose values are like one's own.

Call the formula Answer A. It is not a perfect answer to the questions of professionalism, institutions, and power. Often, of course, the goals and values around which institutions turn are hidden ones; and at best, a morally alive person will hardly ever find an institution whose values seem more than approximately right. Moreover, institutions must balance budgets, and they have a habit of doing so in ways which interfere with making professional services available to all who need them. Usually this means an institution has a social class character.

Simply aligning oneself with a "Christian" institution is no easy solution, for class influence and power may saturate the air

---

Young social workers, doctors, lawyers, and teachers often drive into the inner city or have clients from the inner city visit their offices downtown. These professionals work daily with the dispossessed, but when it comes to being neighbors to them and going to church with them on Sundays, they suddenly fade away. There seems to be a new elitism emerging in the professional world which says, "We stop at the office door." Very few graduates from Protestant seminaries even entertain the idea of an urban parish ministry. Here the Catholic Church has a glowing record of faithfulness when compared to the abysmal flight of the Protestant churches from our inner cities.

My work offers one of the most challenging and exciting career opportunities today. The mix of people and the miracles of God are at times excruciatingly painful, but always exciting and encouraging. If professionals do not serve in the inner city, we will generate a new class of the elite within the church who will become more and more out of touch with the majority of our urban and Third World population. If professional training does not equip us for better servanthood in the humility and spirit of Christ, then professionalism is leading us down a dangerous path of irrelevance and stratification within the church.

one breathes even there. Well-intentioned managers and economists in a Mennonite foundation may justify patterns of accumulation that are in themselves unjust. Professionals in "Christian" hospitals can easily act as if medicine is "high quality" if it offers elaborate, intensive care to those with severe ailments (and the means to pay), forgetting to calculate the extent of the hospital's and their own emphasis on prevention. Church college faculties must consider that, despite a lot of religious talk, their main function might be helping upper-middle-class families launch their children into status-conferring careers.

Moreover, professionals in church institutions face dilemmas even when they try to reconcile concerns that are proper. A "Christian hospital" administrator may want to give patients the benefits of every good scientific technique. Yet as a Christian who is sensitive to what happens to the spirit as well as the body, the administrator is careful not to throw the sick and injured into psychological shock by surrounding them with tubes, stainless steel, wiggling screens, and other frightening gadgetry. Working in a "Christian" institution does not deliver the administrator from the dilemma.

Yet, Answer A is one answer. "Christian" institutions do not "solve" problems of professionalism, institutions, and power. But they are settings where people with kingdom values can become discerning communities that work prayerfully at the issues.

That includes being ready to change some established professional and institutional procedures. Kingdom-minded people may decide that direct fee-for-service arrangements eliminate too many people who really need the services. They will likely work at wiping out big differences in pay for different levels of professionals. And they should do away with pay scales geared more to supporting Acapulco vacations for the professionals than to creating an economic climate that encourages clients to have regular checkups. (For my profession, read "redundant 'educational' travel to Europe or wherever" instead of "Acapulco vacations," and "tuition levels" instead of "an economic climate.")

Answer B: New Institutions

Some kingdom-minded professionals find that certain "Christian" institutions have gotten too rigid and unimaginative, that they are run by hidden goals and distorted values. Or they find them inadequate, or at the wrong places. Such professionals may try to create new institutions.

For example, some Mennonite educators explored creative ways to put Christian thought in front of society's thinkers; the result was the establishing of a Mennonite "satellite" college on a secular university campus in Ontario named after an earlier university student, Conrad Grebel. Some Mennonite health professionals who wanted their services to be more preventive and accessible, and their own worship and lifestyle to reflect their faith, established a close-fellowship church in a poor region of southern Indiana—a kind of village for living—and a group practice organized somewhat differently from the usual medical association's ways. This "new institution" answer to questions of professionalism, power, institutions, and kingdom values, we can call Answer B. Answer B will not necessarily "solve" problems more easily than Answer A, for new institutions can quickly develop the same dilemmas that face old ones. Yet, for some, Answer B may be best.

Answer C: Secular Institutions

Another answer, call it C, is for Christian professionals to pursue their professions within the institutions of society at-large—and then become "creative subversives." Become professionalism, power, institutions, and kingdom values, we ing professions into enemies of the kingdom. Did not Jesus tell us to be wise as serpents while we're harmless as doves?

If Christian professionals are to serve all who need their skills, they need resources beyond what institutions under Christians' control can possibly provide. Government especially can often mobilize resources in ways that private institutions cannot, to serve across social class lines. In proper contexts Christian professionals may deliberately choose to work in governmental institutions. (The "proper contexts" test applies to private institutions as well.) Surely "Christian" institutions, old or new, cannot and should not try to be the only places of kingdom work. I remember counseling a colleague, one very valuable to Goshen College, to leave for a major state university if a certain post opened. He and his spouse were the kind who, if they found no real church, would soon precipitate one. And they would certainly turn a secular university post into an occasion for the highest kind of Christian dialogue with thoughtful worldlings. Answer C is theologically sound. Christians entering the professions in the secular institutions that surround them really represent in microcosm God's placing his church into the world. At least if those Christians go with the support of the church. Yet a strong danger under Answer C can be for the lone follower of Jesus to sally forth at full tilt against professionalism's monsters, only to disappear into a dragon's belly.

The follower of Jesus who goes into the professions, ready to judge practices he finds there by kingdom values, must have a church to help discern what kingdom values mean. Some of us repeat what is by now almost a cliché: "The great temptation is to let the professional peer group be one's church—that is, the reference group for personal identity, for lifestyle, for ethics, and for truth." But it is not a cliché; it is a truism. Actually it is just as true for those who choose A and B as for those who choose C. Indeed, followers of A and B face a subtler temptation: to think that because one's small circle of professional colleagues is devoted to the kingdom, one does not need the rest of the church.

Whatever the temptations, we Christians need not treat professionalism as if it were necessarily an outgrowth of humanity's fall. Certain professions, if built around violent coercion and power, or other sub-Christian principles, do come from the fall. All tendencies to make professionalism into one more instrument to manipulate people and seek status are also associated with the fall.

Nevertheless we may see professionalism itself as neutral, or even growing out of God's good creation. We must keep its values and its confidence in human technique from becoming the ultimate guiding values of our lives. There are ways to work at bringing professionalism's power and its institutions together with kingdom values. There are ways to work at removing barriers that come between professionals and those whom they should serve.

The three answers, A, B, and C, are not solutions but they are three legitimate ways to answer the question.

CHAPTER SEVENTEEN

Celebrating Success?

By S. Dale High

S. Dale High is a Mennonite businessman from Lancaster, Pennsylvania. In his late thirties, he is president of High Industries, the parent company of three groups of subsidiaries: steel, concrete, and real estate and construction. He is active in community organizations, serving presently as chairman of the Lancaster Chamber of Commerce and Industry and on the board of Elizabethtown College.

He spoke with the editors about some of the lines he has drawn in his business life and especially about a matter troubling to many sensitive professionals: "Dare I Celebrate Success?"

Some time ago a pastor came to me and wanted to use my story as an example that if you live right, you become successful. I refused. I don't see it as a cause and effect kind of thing.

I think God cares about the people at High Industries, Inc. I think he cares about the kind of organization it is, whether we commit ourselves to excellence instead of mediocrity—but not what our bottom line is this year. Who knows? We may not be here ten years from now. But I do need to be responsible for the thousand people who work here.

I think business is as much a stewardship profession as any other. It's careful use of resources. I think that's spiritual. I have certain fiduciary problems as an employer. I'm working with the resources of a thousand people's lives. Now you can't impose your value system on them necessarily, although they are affected by it indirectly. For instance, we have tried not to be involved with the military. Recently a strong company approached us who wanted us to build and lease a large munitions plant in one of our industrial parks. While the economics of this might look tempting in a recession year, we turned them down. I thought the company representative was a little cold to me after that, but we stuck with our decision. Later I asked him to serve on a community organization with me. He seemed surprised, but agreed to.

I'm more concerned about making our organization humane, rather than Christian. In fact, in many ways, we don't like to be characterized as a Christian or Mennonite business. We do not operate a Mennonite chapel. We try, instead, to create an atmosphere where people whose values are very different can work together to reach common work goals.

Any success I've been part of has always been a group success. It's never private. I'm a people person. Maybe that's the reason I have the theology I do. I don't know which emanates from which.

I think my wife, Dawn, and I tend to gravitate more toward people who have some Mennonite connections for friendships and support. In fact, we've been part of a fellowship group of church people for about nine years and they're very important to us. Yet I enjoy the Chamber group and the YPO (Young Presidents' Organization, a club for corporate presidents under age forty). I've learned that people other than our own are spiritual. I worked with an attorney one day who had all the usual problems; he had gone through a divorce, etc. And I asked him if we could do something in a particular way. "You could," he said tentatively, "but there's a higher way." Wow, that really struck me. That's spiritual!

So every day you're with people who are better at something than you are. You're never 100 percent successful. I consider Dawn as successful as I am. I try not to take myself too seriously.

I have to be careful that I don't become isolated from people, from social need. That's why I've tried to stay close to community organizations like United Way and the Urban League. Recently one of our black employees who has been with us for a long time wanted to start a new, risky business. He was gathering a total of $65,000 to invest. One evening I went to Baltimore with him and his wife to talk to the party he was considering becoming involved with. I could ask some questions he couldn't. I didn't have time for that, but I took time. There are hundreds of occasions when I haven't taken time, but this time I did.

Time is an endless difficulty. So is lifestyle. It's a continual dilemma. It's unsolved. We went to a YPO meeting a while ago for which we moved from place to place. I was driving a small-size white Buick in the middle of a whole string of black Cadillacs. I enjoyed it. I have a sense of doing without things even though we could afford them.

I think I was the first Mennonite member of the Hamilton Club. We don't participate actively in all its social functions, but it's nice as a place to take other corporate presidents.

At the same time I try to keep in touch with the first line people here (High Industries). We had a union drive recently. That kind of exposure keeps you from getting jaded. Once when I was down in the plant meeting with a group of men, this punk kid sat in the front row. He was downright rude. Every time I'd answer a question, he'd laugh. I wanted to pound him! I thought about that a lot afterward. That was good for me.

What will I tell my kids? Life is broad and joyful. It's easy to become consumed by the business. Success as a person is not succeeding in one area. What society happens to put high priority on—don't be taken in by that. Feel good about whatever you can do well.

Questions of
Faith and
Professionalism

CHAPTER EIGHTEEN

Are Traditional Mennonite Approaches Adequate?

By Gordon D. Kaufman

Introduction

For too long we Mennonites have allowed the modern world simply to overtake us, and have not attempted carefully and intelligently to assess what was happening. In consequence, for the past two generations there has been a steady flow of our young people from the rural communities in which they were raised into cities where they have been swallowed up and lost. Even though we have established churches in many of the larger cities to which Mennonites have gone, we have seldom systematically reflected on the question of what happens to the traditional Mennonite style of life and ethics in a modern urban environment. So our urban churches have been, as far as possible, simply transplanted rural Mennonite churches in character and quality; or they have taken over, rather unthinkingly, patterns of life and ministry from other groups with quite different understandings of Christian faith than those characteristic of Mennonites. The question of how the Mennonite interpretation of Christian faith can be relevant to modern urban and professional life has seldom been faced directly.

I want to acknowledge immediately that I am no expert on this problem. I am a Christian theologian of Mennonite background who has lived most of his life largely outside of Mennonite community circles, one who has been involved, as a professional, in American university education. This background (as a Mennonite), this vocation (reflecting on the meaning of Christian faith), this experience (as a member of a major "profession" in modern America), and my personal concern about the meaning of the Mennonite heritage in the modern world are my only qualifications for speaking to this subject. My own ideas here should be treated as, at best, just tentative formulations of what seem to me to be some of the problems confronted by bearers of the Mennonite heritage when they move into the modern professional world.

I do not intend in this essay to take up the problems of particular professions, or to give a profile of what modern professionalism is all about. I shall confine myself to the attempt to isolate and analyze certain features of our Mennonite heritage which present particular problems for those moving into the highly educated modern professional world. And I shall attempt to suggest the sort of reformulation of Mennonite-Christian faith that seems necessary if we are to adequately meet these issues.

The Mennonite Problem

How does it happen that there is a special problem for Mennonites who become professionals? What sort of problem is it? I am no sociologist, but I think some sociological remarks might be in order here to set the stage for our more theological considerations. Throughout most of their history, Mennonites (excepting those in Holland) have lived in relatively closed, relatively small rural communities. Everyone knew everyone else; everyone lived substantially the same style of life, faced the same problems, cherished the same values. Though some Mennonites went into so-called helping professions like teaching or medicine, these seemed to be direct expressions of the basic Mennonite understanding that life is to be devoted to the service of one's fellow human beings. Certainly, the beginnings of professionalized life in small communities did not seem to raise serious questions with the Mennonite communal ethic.

The situation for those of us in modern urban professions is very different from this. We no longer live as members of relatively closed, small communities, sharing a common ethos and lifestyle with all our neighbors; we are now more or less isolated individuals in large cities, working in a variety of vocations, including highly specialized professions, and dealing with increasingly complex, unprecedented problems. Most of our contacts are with others who do not share our understanding of Christian faith and who may be pursuing very different values than we think appropriate. The problems on which we and our colleagues in the several professions have to make decisions raise issues that human beings have never thought of before, and for which our traditional Mennonite ethic has given us virtually no preparation at all. If we are physicians, we must concern ourselves with questions like when, and under what circumstances, it is right for us to perform abortions, or whether our patient is truly "dead," so that it is legitimate to remove an organ for transplant. If we are lawyers or politicians, we must be prepared to write and assess laws that will define under what circumstances that abortion will be legitimate and legal, or how certain businesses ought to be regulated so as to protect consumers, or what American policy ought to be with regard to Israel or South Africa. If we are in business, we must face the question whether all investments are equally legitimate, what degree and kind of "truth" we will present in our advertising, what kind of labor policies are appropriate and just in today's world. One could go on and on. Whether we are architects, teachers, psychiatrists, or bankers, new and exceedingly difficult moral dilemmas are bound to face us. For many of these our traditional Mennonite background has given us no preparation whatsoever. Moreover, for many of these our fellow professionals have no more wisdom than we on how to proceed.

The problem is more acute for us Mennonites than for many of our professional friends, however, because of a peculiarity of the Mennonite consciousness: the notion of the church as set over against the world. Mennonites have what the sociologists often call a sectarian consciousness. We tend to see the world outside the church as sinful, fallen, dangerous; it is inside the Christian community that right and truth are to be found, and it is from the Christian community, therefore, that one is to take one's principal orientation in life. This sort of closed-group consciousness worked satisfactorily as long as Mennonites lived in relatively closed communities where they could insulate themselves fairly successfully from the outside world. But in modern professional life it makes no sense at all. Our lives are lived for the most part outside the confines of the church. Our professional education is acquired from schools that have little interest in or knowledge of Mennonite traditions, and that means that the very form of our professional life will be "worldly." Almost everything we do as professionals we do as participants in secular institutions that have little or no interest in the church. It is therefore impossible for modern Mennonite professionals to live the church-world dualism which characterized an earlier period of Mennonite history. If we are going to be professionals today, our lives will be lived "in the world" in a much fuller sense than many earlier Mennonites would have regarded as legitimate, and the norms and standards with which we make decisions in our professions will be drawn from our experience in the world. The major sociological assumptions on which earlier formulations of Mennonite faith were based simply do not hold true for modern professional life.

Does this mean that if one is to be a professional in the modern world one cannot be a loyal Mennonite? Or that if one is a convinced Mennonite, he or she dare not go into a modern profession?

The Erosion of Biblical Authority

The problems which our Mennonite heritage poses as we confront the modern professional world go considerably deeper than the much too simple church-world dualism I have just mentioned. They are rooted, I think, in some of the most fundamental Mennonite convictions about the foundations of our moral knowledge, in our understanding of life itself.

Most human beings seldom ask questions about where their moral ideas and insights come from. We acquire ideals of honesty, loyalty, justice, and mercy along with a great deal else in the way of knowledge, habits, and skills as we grow through childhood and adolescence to maturity. For the most part human values and ideals are learned in the family and in the immediate community in which one grows up. The tradition which informs the life and institutions of that community becomes the tradition which we make our own and thus which comes to orient our life. This is true whether we are Americans or Chinese, Christians or Hindus, Mennonites or Jews or secularists. As long as it is possible for a community to maintain patterns of life similar to those which had been followed in the past, the tradition can remain viable and significant as a means of orientation for members of the community, and it is not necessary to search for new standards or values to guide one's decisions. Moral practice and understanding can follow long-tested habitual patterns.

It is when persons encounter quite new situations, forcing them to deal with unprecedented problems, that the tradition gets called into question. At those moments where the traditional maxims and habits no longer seem to apply, one is forced to ask in a new way about right and wrong, what shall I do, how shall I plot my course. Then one moves back to what one believes to be the sources of moral insight or moral understanding in order to gain a standing place from which to address the new and complex issues. Perhaps one will turn to the philosophical tradition of moral reflection, to see what can be learned there about rightness and goodness and justice. Or perhaps one will turn within, listening for a clearer word from the voice of conscience. Or again: one may turn to others alleged to be wise persons—counselors, pastors, teachers—who may give one guidance.

For Mennonites, the source of moral insight and understanding has been believed to be the Scripture. The Bible, and particularly the teachings of Jesus, have been thought to present the very "word of God," the absolute truth about right and wrong, the perfect norm for ordering all of human life. When traditional patterns and practices no longer seemed relevant, therefore, Mennonites have believed they should turn back to the Scripture to resolve their problems. Here they would find guidance enabling them to deal with the new issues which faced them.

Thus, the basic Mennonite orientation in life has been *authoritarian.* Mennonites have believed that there is an absolute authority which can and does provide sufficient guidance for every situation and condition into which a human might fall. Life is based first of all on the authority of tradition, and when the traditional patterns prove to be no longer adequate, one turns back to the absolute authority of Scripture to resolve problems. We are inclined to ask, "Are there any biblical principles that apply to professionalism?" Mennonites have come almost instinctively to approach new problems with that sort of question.

Now I want to suggest that the movement into professional life is one which calls into question—perhaps renders obsolete—precisely this traditional Mennonite turning to authority, as the appropriate way to deal with new problems in life. The simple and straightforward Mennonite beliefs about the Bible's authority are called into question in at least two ways for those who have a modern professional education. In the first place, a member of a modern profession will ordinarily have a liberal arts college education and several years of university training beyond that. Such a person, knowing something of modern history and science, will be aware that the Bible was produced in a culture very different from our own, that it presents many ideas about the world, about human existence, about the movements of history, that we can only regard as mythical, and that it is in many respects a culturally relative product of a particular segment of human history. However important the Bible may have been as formative of Western culture—and it was very important indeed—any modern educated person now sees it as relative and limited in many respects.

Aware as we are of the at least equal importance that Greek

traditions have had in forming our culture, and of the several other religiocultural traditions which humankind has produced around the world, it becomes increasingly difficult to regard the Bible as the kind of absolute authority which it was for our parents and grandparents. The very education which one undergoes in preparing for a modern profession tends to undercut, or call into question, the relatively naive belief in biblical authority which has characterized much Mennonite faith. One begins to wonder in what sense, and why, one can claim this particular document to be somehow the very "Word of God," having a kind of absoluteness that other monuments of ancient wisdom cannot claim.

It is not his or her education alone, however, which tends to erode biblical authority for the modern professional. Even more serious is the fact that the Bible seems to have no clear word on many of the important issues that one has to face in one's professional life. Doubtless the biblical principle of loving one's neighbor is of great importance: but what specific guidance does this give the social worker in counseling a thirteen-year-old girl on whether she should abort the three-month-old fetus that she is carrying? Of what help can the Bible be to a mortgage officer of a bank when he is attempting to formulate investment policy? What biblical principles are to be invoked if I am attempting to decide whether or not to give my life to the study of astronomy? Does the principle of love of enemy provide any specific guidance to a lawyer who has been asked to sue an unscrupulous landlord on behalf of a tenant whose apartment has been left unrepaired? The problems with which members of modern professions must deal most of the time simply were not addressed by the writers of the Bible, because they are problems that arise from a completely different cultural situation, one that those writers could never have imagined. Whatever overriding moral and religious significance the teachings of the Bible may have had for earlier generations, it is not at all clear how the Bible can remain authoritative in the day-to-day decisions of the lives of most Americans in professions.

In consequence of these two considerations—on the one hand, our increasing awareness of the actual historical process which produced the Bible and its consequent cultural relativity, and on the other hand, our increasing experience of complex and difficult moral issues to which the Bible does not seem to speak at all—biblical authority over the whole of life tends inevitably to become seriously eroded for anyone in a modern profession. Therefore as long as Mennonites insist on framing their interpretation of Christian faith in authoritarian terms, they will be in serious trouble in dealing with problems of modern urban life. An authoritarian approach to the problems of faith and life works as long as the authority is both unquestioned and obviously relevant. When either or both of those conditions is eroding away, the authoritarian approach itself is in serious danger and must be replaced by some other. If the only truly relevant and informed approach to the actual questions with which one has to deal is that found in professional journals or the public press, it is to them that the concerned person will have to turn. And with that turning, one leaves the Mennonite tradition one step further behind.

As you can see, I do not think traditional Mennonitism, rooted as it is in biblical authoritarianism, is equipped to deal with problems faced by persons in modern professions. If our Mennonite-Christian faith is to have a bearing on these issues, its very foundations must be reformulated. I would like to propose such a reformulation now.

 ## Beyond Authoritarianism

The fact that we can no longer work out of an authoritarian biblical ethic does not mean that all that we have learned under the tutelage of that ethic is invalid. On the contrary, I am prepared to argue that the understanding of human life, its central problems, and the treatment for those problems, which Mennonites have gained from the Bible—particularly from the teachings and example of Jesus—remain valid and true, and can be the basis for dealing with problems arising in the modern professions. The professions are, after all, attempting in some way to deal with the meaning and fulfillment of human life, and any insight that can be thrown on those questions will be of immense importance in setting directions and proposing objectives for the professions.

There are three things particularly about the Mennonite-Christian understanding of the nature and meaning of human existence that I want to emphasize here. First, that human life is primarily communitarian. Human beings are not isolated atoms who can and should live unto themselves and can find fulfillment by themselves; we are members one of another, and human life finds its fulfillment in the love and trust and mutual support experienced in community.

Second, genuine community is no easy achievement among human beings, each of whom is striving to gain his or her own private objectives. Rather, it is created only through the willingness of selves to sacrifice themselves for others in ministries of reconciliation and forgiveness and service, ministries that extend not only to those with whom we are in agreement but even to our enemies. The willingness to give oneself in love to one's enemies, even as Jesus gave himself on the cross, is the only kind of stance that will make possible the building of true community among humans.

Third, human life is life "under God." That is, human beings, neither as individuals nor as communities, exist simply of themselves or for themselves, but they have their lives from beyond themselves, and they can find genuine fulfillment only in significant relation to that ultimate source of their being which we call God. Life oriented toward self, life oriented toward our community or nation, even life oriented toward the good of all humanity has ultimately too narrow a focus. It is idolatrous, and as such stultifying and destructive, not only of ourselves and our fellow humans, but also of the rest of life and, indeed, of all of creation—as the ecologists are daily reminding us. If we are to live in harmony and peace with our neighbors and with the rest of creation, we must learn to devote ourselves to that one who creates and sustains us all.

These notions of love and self-sacrifice, reconciliation and community, devotion and service to God, which have been of importance to Mennonites (as well as other Christians) were learned by them under tutelage of biblical authority. And many Mennonites, I suppose, take these to be important only because they are taught in the Bible. That authoritarian position, however, is not the only possible one. It is also possible to hold to these convictions simply because one believes them to be true—true, that is, to what human nature actually is, true to the human condition, a true understanding of human problems.

We are human beings, each of us, and we are daily in contact with other human beings. On the basis of our experience, and our insight into that experience, we may see how important it is for humans to love each other, to forgive each other, to live in community with each other, to worship only that God who is beyond all the idols which attract us. In that case these things are now affirmed and believed and practiced because our own insight and understanding and experience show us their significance and truth. Here it is our own understanding and insight that have become authoritative for us, the guide and basis of our judgments in life; we have moved beyond dependence on the external authority of the Bible. We are still affirming a Mennonite-Christian ethic and faith, but no longer one based simply on authoritarian foundations.

It is this kind of Mennonite approach to the problems of the vocations that I would advocate. When we recognize that our decisions will have to be based on our own insight and understanding, that we cannot depend for final answers on authorities who simply give them to us, but must take responsibility for ourselves and our judgments and our decisions, we will move to a new level of maturity. We will be open to facing whatever issues and problems confront us, examining them in their own terms, and working out as best we can a responsible approach to them. We will be prepared to learn from other professionals what they have to teach us about the issues which we must face together with them, but we will not find ourselves impelled simply to take over what they say without careful scrutiny in terms of our understanding of what human life is really all about.

This does not mean that we will find easy answers to the questions we confront. But it does mean we can openly and straightforwardly confront any question we encounter, whether there are relevant biblical teachings with regard to it or not, whether Mennonites have ever looked at that issue before or not.

The approach which I am advocating allows a kind of openness and freedom in addressing problems which is virtually unlimited. It allows us—indeed, it requires us—even to be willing to question our own principles, lest they become idols which we serve instead of God. Take, for example, the central Mennonite belief that serving others, nonresistance, should characterize our every stance in life. However significant and true this Mennonite belief in self-sacrifice may seem to us, it is important for us to consider carefully the kind of evidence that persons like Nietzsche and Freud have produced against it. It seems clear that attitudes and practices of self-sacrifice are often engendered by fear instead of love, and that they can have as their consequence repressed hostility, which is anything but forgiving. All of us know from our own experience, I suspect, how frequently the tight-lipped martyr is to be found in the typical Mennonite community. Supposing it immoral ever to express hatred or hostility, many Mennonite communities are filled with tensions, bitterness, backbiting, and secret struggles for power. If the Mennonite emphasis on love and reconciliation is to be maintained, it will have to be qualified by a careful appropriation of what modern psychiatry can teach us about the deviousness and the depths of human selves.

Other examples of the way in which our conceptions of human life and its fulfillment must be brought into confrontation with other traditions and points of view in the modern world could be cited: the significance of the body and of human sexuality has been little understood in traditional Mennonitism; the role of power in human institutions, including our own Men-

nonite institutions, has been systematically obscured; the need
for beauty, and the importance of the arts in a fulfilled human
life, has simply not been realized.

On these and many other questions about human life, and
what human life is all about, the Bible has no clear answers, and
to insist on biblicism would itself be idolatrous. We must take the
responsibility for our judgments on ourselves, relying on our own
insight, understanding, and experience, to find such answers as
we can live by and work with. We must be prepared to open up
our Mennonitism to attitudes and practices unknown or even re-
jected in the past, in order to help enable it to become a vital and
significant force in the new situation in the present in which we
are living and into which we are moving.

There is, of course, some point at which transformation of
the tradition has become so drastic and far-reaching that it is no
longer recognizably Mennonite. Each of us would probably
mark that point somewhat differently, but for all of us it is there.
For my part, I would define this point, not in terms of any
idiosyncratic details of Mennonite custom or consciousness, but
in terms of the central vision of the human, and the fulfillment of
the human, which has gripped the Mennonite consciousness: that
it is in relationships of love and trust and self-giving in the recon-
ciling community that true humanity is realized, and that the
image of Jesus in ministry, teaching, and death is the criterion or
paradigm in terms of which this conception of the human is
concretely pictured and defined. So long as we hold to this, it
seems to me, we are maintaining what is truly important in historic Mennonitism.

An approach such as I am suggesting here leaves us open to
deal with whatever problems arise in the course of our
professional lives. Recognizing that there are no "prepackaged"
answers to the moral and religious questions we are facing and
will face, we must take responsibility upon ourselves to work out
such answers as we can find. This is, so far as I can see, the only
way it will be possible to be a Mennonite in a modern profession.
In Philippians 2 Paul makes a similar point. First he commends

the example of Jesus who, "... though he was in the form of God, did not count equality with God a thing to be grasped, but emptied himself, taking the form of a servant" (Phil. 2:6, 7, RSV). Then he suggests that the Philippians must now "... work out your own salvation with fear and trembling; for God is at work in you, both to will and to work for his good pleasure" (2:12, 13). In the last analysis, in Paul's view, even with the biblical image of true humanity before us, we must ourselves take responsibility for how this applies to our own situation, and we must act on that responsibility.

The very open and unstructured interpretation of Mennonitism in the face of modern professional life, which I am proposing, is frightening and it will be difficult to execute. It is frightening because it admits openly that there is no authority to which we can turn to resolve our most difficult moral and religious problems; it acknowledges that we must take full responsibility on ourselves in these matters. It is difficult to execute because the lack of ultimate authority means there are no clear guidelines to be followed; we will have to find our own way, and that will require both considerable time and effort and may be frustrating and exhausting.

But there are resources to which we can turn for help in our reflection: above all, the picture of Jesus which we find in the Scriptures is such a resource, providing illumination of the nature and problems of human life and of the will of God whom we worship. The long history of Christian reflection on the meaning of Jesus' life, teachings, and death can provide important guidance and help in grasping the full significance of this figure central to Christian faith. Philosophical reflection on ethical issues may give us insight into important dimensions of the problems we face, and sociological analyses and literary portrayals of the complexity and problems of modern urban civilization will surely sharpen our discernment and deepen our understanding of the many layers and dimensions of the moral and religious issues with which we must deal.

Finally, the efforts of some of our contemporaries in the

professions in which we are living and working, to discern and interpret the moral issues at stake in the major questions facing the profession, will surely be of help. We must draw on all these resources and any others which become available to us as we seek to develop our own insight and understanding so that we can decide and act wisely and responsibly.

Communities of Discernment

If we were to attempt to go this route simply as individuals—and that is what has been forced onto many of us—I suspect we would lose our Mennonitism in the end. If not we ourselves, then our children would. There is, however, an alternative to a strictly individualistic approach, an alternative suggested by our Mennonite heritage itself. We can band together in the cities as small Mennonite communities, communities of fellow-seekers, fellow-professionals, attempting to support and help each other. If we could find a way to organize our urban churches as genuine "communities of discernment," which would seek to help their members more adequately face the unprecedented problems and decisions which modern professionals must address, there would be some chance that in the brave new world into which we are moving we would not simply become lost.

We all need a group with whom we can share our deepest and most destructive dilemmas; we need a group so open and nonjudgmental that we can bring our most secret doubts and questions for discussion and consideration; we need a fellowship of love and trust where we need not deceive or cover up any of the issues that we encounter as we try to bring to bear the understanding of human existence which we have inherited from our Mennonite tradition on the problems we face in our modern professions. All too often, I fear, our Mennonite churches have been anything but open communities of this sort of love and trust. But in such open communities it might be possible for us to find truly significant Mennonite ways to face the problems posed by modern urban life. Participation in such communities might enable us finally to grow out of that childish immaturity that must always live from parental or traditional authority, gradually learning to take full responsibility for ourselves, our beliefs, and our actions. We would then "... no longer ... be children" but would be moving into ... "mature manhood, measured by nothing less than the full stature of Christ" (Eph. 4:13, 14, NEB).

CHAPTER NINETEEN

Is the Bible a Relevant Resource?

By Marlin E. Miller

The Gap Between Yesterday and Today

Many Christian professionals perceive a fundamental discontinuity between the Bible and today's world. The realities of which the Scriptures speak appear shrouded in the gathering mists of an antiquated past. Complex contemporary social organizations have replaced the apparently simple social organization of biblical times. Modern urban values and lifestyles have superseded the agrarian lifestyles and values of Jesus' day. Technological advances have fundamentally diminished fearful dependency on overpowering forces of nature. Scientific analysis of the world and human experience have challenged and ostensibly rendered traditional belief systems obsolete. If today's world seemingly shares so little with the world of the Bible, can the Scriptures remain the unique guide and foundational resource for Christian faith and life in our time?

Mennonite professionals in particular may sense an even greater distance between the New Testament and contemporary society. The Anabaptist emphasis on following Christ in all of life has depended on biblical standards of discipleship and moral judgment. But how does biblical nonresistance apply to the exercise of power in legal and business professions? What guidance do the Scriptures offer on whether and under what conditions medical doctors should discontinue medical support systems for dying patients? Are there biblical perspectives which can or should inform the decisions and priorities of Mennonite social workers? Besides participating in the broader movement from rural to urban society and from traditional to modern ways of thinking, Mennonite professionals face choices and challenges for which there often seem to be few or no relevant biblical answers.

For Mennonite professionals, this apparent distance and discontinuity between the Bible and today's world is reinforced by the presumed synthesis between the ethnic Mennonitism of the last generation and the Bible. The traditional Mennonite way supposedly fit the biblical standards like a well-tailored coat. Church discipline and minimal involvement in the broader society made litigation irrelevant as well as morally prohibited. Rural, general practitioners didn't face the complex ethical issues of technological medical care. But as Mennonites move into the professions and urban society, the previously experienced harmony between a Mennonite subculture and the Bible has been at least threatened, if not stymied. The distance and discontinuity between modern professional life and traditional Mennonite mores has thus been projected onto the difference between contemporary urban society and the biblical world. The cultural and ethical irrelevance of traditional ethnic Mennonitism to contemporary professional life has been transferred to the Bible.

The question of whether the Bible is a foundational resource and guide for Mennonite professionals can be looked at fairly only by simultaneously distinguishing between rural ethnic Mennonitism and a renewed biblical vision of discipleship. We first need to differentiate between our perceptions of traditional Mennonitism and our approach to biblical discipleship. In other words, leaving ethnic Mennonitism "back on the farm" doesn't necessarily confirm the "irrelevance" of the Bible for Christian professionals.

The Overlap of Subculture and Biblical Interpretation

We have often identified traditional Mennonitism with biblical discipleship. That skews our perception of the Bible as a unique guide for Christians in modern professions.

Traditional Mennonitism often became a provincial subculture which imposed its standards by an authoritarian appeal to the Scriptures. Attempts to debate or deviate were, on occasion, squelched by a contrived appeal to favorite proof texts. This uncritical identification of the subculture with the biblical standards also implied that the Bible offered little or no guidance for living "outside" the Mennonite subculture "in the world." When some left for a career in nontraditional Mennonite professions, they quite logically expected little biblical direction. They had learned their lesson well—and they accepted the message: The Scriptures are largely "irrelevant" to living in the "world" outside a Mennonite subculture.

Moreover, identifying biblical discipleship with traditional Mennonite mores often contributed to the belief that the Bible is a unique guide and foundational resource, giving explicit directives and universally applicable principles for *all* of life. If, however, the Scriptures offer no explicit instructions for many issues in modern medical technology, in financial management, or in legal practice, can they remain the normative guide for Christian discipleship? Certain forms of traditional Mennonitism may assume that the Bible's authority and relevance is diminished if it does not provide explicit answers or an obvious consensus on complex contemporary questions. This assumption has more to do with a style of biblical interpretation than with the Bible as a foundational resource. It points toward the need for an alternate method and context of interpretation, which allows the Bible to function as a critical norm and ordering principle of Christian professional life.

The failure to distinguish between a Mennonite subculture and the biblical context may also contribute to a sense of distance between the Bible and contemporary issues. Many Mennonite professionals perceive a discontinuity between ethnic Mennonites and life in the late twentieth century. And that may affect how they see the historical context of the Bible in relation to the modern world. On the other hand, instead of diminishing the relevance of the Scriptures, that distance can be a critical instrument to distinguish ethnic Mennonitism from formative biblical perspectives. It can also be an interpretative instrument for discerning analogous patterns of belief and life in today's setting without rationalizing our thoughts and actions as unquestionably biblical and therefore in no need of continuing discernment and prayer.

Modern professionals may feel that as contemporary Christians they have more in common with the modern world than with the church throughout history. The Bible is hardly the book of contemporary Western society. Seen in the perspective of general historical consciousness, the Bible belongs to a past period in human history. The discontinuity between the modern and the ancient world would in this view supersede the continuity of the Christian church through the ages. The question is, however, whether those who confess Jesus as Messiah and Lord find their primary historical identity in the Christian community, which reaches back to the New Testament churches, or primarily in the communities of modern professional guilds.

Thus, traditionalistic Mennonite biblical interpretation has likely contributed as much to the assumption that the Scriptures offer little guidance for Christians in modern professions as has contemporary society's disregard for the Bible. The lack of explicit biblical directives for all significant ethical decisions does not in itself make the Bible less relevant for Christian professionals, unless relevancy is defined primarily in terms of explicit moral rules and policies. That the biblical writings were first addressed to Christians of other cultures can enhance their use for discerning the direction of Christian life and witness in our time, rather than making them less relevant. The Christian church as the confessing community, rather than a particular cultural epoch, should constitute the primary frame of reference for Christian identity and the primary context in which the Bible is interpreted and contemporary issues confronted. An authentic biblical authority becomes useful as the Scriptures provide the foundation for responding to the values, insights, and practices of the modern world as well as of traditional subcultures.

The Archive of Our Witness

The Bible constitutes the normative guide and foundational resource for Christian faith and life because it is the primary and unique witness to Jesus Christ. Throughout the history of the Christian churches, the Bible has been the standard which has preserved the Christian confession of Jesus as the Christ from fragmentation on the one hand and embellishment on the other. Where the Bible has functioned this way in the churches, we find keener moral and spiritual discernment, more authentic church renewal, more vigorous Christian witness, and more significant contributions to the broader culture and society.

As the primary and unique witness to Jesus as the Christ, the Bible becomes the normative guide for Christian life and ethical discernment. This implies that constant recourse to the biblical witness itself rather than to particular theological constructs about the Scriptures remains of primary importance for Christians in general and for Christian professionals in particular. Our theological constructs as well as particular issues need to be tested by continuing to wrestle with the texts themselves. For example, Christian ethical thought has often assumed that the biblical image of Jesus as the Christ is "apolitical" and that therefore the New Testament offers little or no guidance for "political" life. Taking the biblical witness to Jesus Christ as the guide for ethical discernment on its own terms, André Trocmé in *Jesus and the Nonviolent Revolution*, John Howard Yoder in *The Politics of Jesus*, and others have demonstrated its relevance for developing a Christian perspective on politics and an alternate style of political action.

Affirming the Bible as the normative guide and foundational resource for Christian life and thought does not blind Christians to truth and insight from other sources. Indeed, it should encourage Christian professionals in particular to engage in discriminating dialogue and debate with the understandings, values, and practices of modern society. Recent biblical studies have shown that many themes in the Scripture reflect their historical origins but simultaneously reshape those elements as carriers of the biblical message. Biblical scholars have shown, for example, that a variety of legal materials is reflected in Exodus 20 to 23. Some of the legal materials reflect prevailing customs and social differentiation of the time; others a distinctive standard of equality and compassion. In contrast to the ancient Mesopotamian culture which separated civil, moral, and religious codes, the book of the covenant in Exodus brought together moral, cultic, and civil prescriptions. Moreover, God's saving activity was the central dynamic which shaped and reshaped these legal materials into a distinctive code for ordering anew the life of God's people. In a similar fashion, the Bible can function as the normative guide as Christians confront, critique, adapt, and reshape concepts, values, and practices which communicate the distinctiveness of Christian faith and practice in our time.

Jacques Ellul illustrates in some measure this effort in a French Protestant setting. His writings seek to articulate a distinctively Christian witness in the modern world. The Scriptures function as the normative guide for his dialogue and debate with contemporary culture and society. In this way Ellul avoids both a strictly intra-church monologue as well as a benign adaptation to the spirit of the age. In *The Presence of the Kingdom,* he outlines what he considers the unique tasks of Christian intellectuals and professionals in the modern world. Many of his writings are set in tandem: for example, his sociological diagnosis of *The Technological Society* is the companion volume to his biblical interpretation of contemporary society in *The Meaning of the City.* Those of Anabaptist persuasion will miss the constitutive reality of Christian community in Ellul's vision. And his ethics may reflect his radical Calvinist heritage more than a consistently Anabaptist stance. Nevertheless he offers a significant model as an intellectual and a professional who takes the Bible seriously as normative guide and foundational resource.

Finally, accepting the Scriptures as normative also implies remembering that the Bible is a missionary document rather than the charter of a professional guild. As such, it has a particular bias. Mennonite professionals who are moving from agrarian and traditional to urban and cosmopolitan settings may tend to forget this bias. But the New Testament writings in particular arose in the context of mission. They don't speak to maintaining the self-interest of a particular group nor to smooth adaptations from rural to urban culture. They focus rather on the ever renewed call of God's people in a variety of historical and cultural contexts to witness in word and deed to salvation, justice, and reconciliation in Jesus Christ. They reflect the bias that "being his witness" constitutes the primary vocation of Christians in the world. This can hardly be construed to mean that Christian professionals in general, or Mennonite professionals in particular, will have "all the right answers" for their specific professions. But it should mean an ordering of priorities in which the vocation of Christian witness takes precedence over professional demands, values, and role expectations.

Interpretation in Community

If the Bible is to function as the foundational resource and unique guide for Christian professionals, they will need the context of a Christian community devoted to biblical interpretation and moral discernment on at least two levels. A local congregation constitutes the primary expression of this process. Second, networks and gatherings of Christian professionals beyond the usual professional organizations provide an additional Christian community.

Boyd Reese (1979:52) rightly proposes that "as professionals, it is crucial that we address the issues with fellow professionals who share our Christian vision.... We need a forum for this. We need to be able to reflect together on issues with our brothers and sisters and seek to break the sovereignty of the powers. In talking with people who understand the profession, we must discern the issues that the profession faces, the issues the profession should face but does not because of its sovereignty, and the issues that face us directly in our practice as professionals...." This kind of common discernment among Christian professionals would provide a setting for dialogue about professional issues and ongoing biblical interpretation. Biblical scholars, theologians, and ethicists could also commit themselves to longer-term dialogue and discernment with such groups of Christians in other professions, rather than remaining within their own boundaries.

Such common discernment among Christian professionals where the Bible functions as a foundational resource need not replace membership in the usual professional organizations and societies. The question is rather one of priorities, namely, that the Christian community takes precedence over other communities in shaping the values, commitments, and actions of those who seek to follow Christ in all of life. The participation or nonparticipation—or the degree of participation in the guild associations—depends on its compatibility with the prior claim of the confessing community.

The other context in which the Bible can function as a normative guide and foundational resource for Christian professionals is the local congregation. Citing Reese (1979:53) again, "Even if our congregation does not have the inside, expert knowledge of the profession, most of us are caught up in involvement in the world in such a way that our experience can throw light on the perplexing decisions our brothers and sisters must face. Again, while we won't be able to share from the perspective of people who have been socialized into the profession, this very fact can be helpful because of the possibility of the input of a perspective that is not bound by the conventional wisdom of our profession." The continuing task of interpreting the Scriptures in the encounter with the contemporary world belongs to this type of moral discernment in a local congregation. But the style of congregational life may need to undergo significant changes in order to function as a community of moral judgment and discriminating biblical interpretation.

In our local Assembly congregation, such a beginning attempt has been made in two ways. In the longer-range worship planning, a series of Sunday services were focused on the issues faced by members of the congregation in several different professions. During this series, the two-and-one-half hour services included open forums, dialogue between persons of various professions, dramatic portrayals of crucial issues, biblical studies related to the themes, and congregational discussion. In addition to the extended series, professionals have been encouraged to share and reflect on their concerns, questions, and insights during the "open sharing time" each Sunday service.

In addition to participating in the Sunday services, all members of the congregation, including "professionals," belong to house meetings which usually meet on a weekly basis. These settings provide a context where members can seek guidance in a continuing manner, where common discernment and scriptural interpretation takes place, and where accountability to discipleship priorities can be combined with mutual support and understanding. On occasion, the "findings" in the house meetings, whether with regard to specific issues or in biblical interpretation in relation to such issues, become a part of the broader congregational agenda.

The Bible can thus function as a foundational resource for Christian professionals to the extent that they allow it to become their normative guide. Moral discernment will be a process in the Christian community as it encounters the contemporary world. For Mennonite professionals in particular, the creation and strengthening of alternate styles of church life may be necessary to enable this interpretive process to happen. And for Mennonite professionals, a "renewing of our minds" may also be needed, lest we assume that the distintegration of rural, ethnic Mennonitism diminishes the relevance of the Scriptures for Christian life in contemporary society.

CHAPTER TWENTY

Is There a Theology for Professionals?

By Gayle Gerber Koontz

The Clash of Vision and Reality

I began my first year of teaching—ninth-grade English in Melrose, Massachusetts—with high hopes as well as with fear and trembling. I intended to be one of those teachers who was also a human being. Believing that Christianity meant following the example of Jesus, I intended to care for and meet the needs of each individual I encountered. I hoped to call forth respect from my students because of my broader knowledge and experience, my genuine concern for their well-being, and my ability to appeal to their rationality. In keeping with my Mennonite concern for nonresistant love and the noncoercive use of power, I preferred not to wield the power of grades or dismissal that were mine simply because I was a teacher in a public school.

One semester, three school dropouts, and numerous class expulsions and student conferences later, I decided that for the sake of the majority of students, certain problem students had to be sacrificed. Coercive power was an unavoidable ingredient in teacher-student relations, and in some cases using it with destructive results for the troublemakers was necessary for the welfare of others.

It was clear to me that I had compromised something that was essential to my understanding of Jesus as peacemaker—he used his power to evoke rather than to force discipleship; he ultimately gave himself up rather than fighting against those who tried to destroy him. Did this imply that as a Christian I could not in good conscience participate in the teaching profession, at least in this public school, because the realities of power prevented me from being a peacemaker? If not, did involvement inevitably mean compromise, falling short of God's intention, in short, necessary failure? Had I misunderstood the example of Jesus? Or was my version of theology too simplistic for our complex, modern world?

I suspect many Mennonite professionals are uneasy with this disjunction between a heritage of nonresistent love with its skepticism of coercion and the ambiguities of power which confront many of us in our work worlds. We find power embedded in client-professional relations. Not only are clients at their most vulnerable moment when they seek the help of a physician, attorney, or psychologist, but professionals wield status, wealth, and privileged knowledge. On the other hand, professionals also feel constricted by the institutions in which they work; they feel their personal identities influenced by their professional associations; and they feel intimidated by an increasingly vocal public which challenges professional assumptions.

As I have continued to explore this apparent tension between our interpretation of Jesus as a pacifist and the way we often find ourselves wielding power in our home, church, and profession, I have learned a great deal from other Christian traditions and friends, as well as from Mennonite colleagues and writers. I do not pretend to have new answers to an old problem, but I would like to sketch a route that might make our theology and experience more compatible.

Keeping Theology Alive

First, I define theology primarily as a *dynamic process* and only secondarily as a particular, substantive system of beliefs. Doing theology means immersing oneself in a conversation between the "stuff" of our everyday experience and the ideas and images central to Christian faith as they have been communicated to us through the Bible and the Christian community. This process is new for every Christian, for each one of us must bring our particular experience into the conversation. The search for a theology that speaks to professionals, then, can never be a task solely or even primarily for "professional" theologians. Each Christian professional must bring to life his or her own system of beliefs which takes the dilemmas and convictions arising from personal experience seriously, and examine them in the light of theological images and ideas. Such a process results in a "living theology." Without attentiveness to experience, and without engagement in such a dynamic process, a Christian will find that any system of beliefs shrivels into meaningless abstraction. Such a theology loses its power to articulate the meaning of God and human existence; it has no relevance to the realities of our professional lives.

Doing Theology with Others

Second, doing theology is *not only a radically individual process, but a radically communal one as well.* Formulating a living theology is necessarily an individual task. But we cannot carry on a theological conversation in a vacuum. With the exception of a few who claim to have experienced direct, unmediated revelations of God, most of us receive the ideas and images of Christian faith through the Bible as it is interpreted by people we know, by theologians and religious leaders, and by the church traditions we have been part of. Some of those images and ideas we find meaningful; others lifeless. But all of them are offered to us by others—the products of others' theological conversations. That communal process is part of the essence of theology. God is revealed not only in Jesus, but in Jesus as he is interpreted in the community of Christians.

I have found the experience of others in the church invaluable in providing balance for my own limited experience. The struggles of others to formulate living theologies have been critical in illuminating and challenging my own. I am persuaded that the Anabaptist-Mennonite conviction that the Word of God is best understood by individuals within the community of believers is a profound one. I think Christians should intentionally seek out communal contexts in which to do theology. For me, however, the community of believers is not a single entity, but rather is made up of circles of the church. It consists of a primary, concrete group of Anabaptists here in Boston and then other concentric circles of the extended community of believers. These circles include not only other Anabaptists (living and dead) but those of diverse Christian traditions, theological assumptions, and economic, national, and racial makeup. While I have chosen to associate with an Anabaptist-Mennonite community as my primary community for theological conversation, I am also convinced that they do not have a corner on revelation!

Updating the Truth

A theological process that expects dynamic interchange between Christian faith and experience within the community of believers rests on a *theology of the Spirit.* Commitment to theology as a process suggests that God is revealed not only in the living theologies of people we encounter in the Bible, particularly in the life and death of Jesus Christ, but also significantly and perhaps in new ways in the continuing life of the community of believers.

As an Anabaptist Mennonite, I take the interpretation of Jesus as a peacemaker as a primary biblical theme. But a theology of conversation recognizes that the Spirit and Word of God continues to unfold as new experience meets this deeply rooted idea and image. We are illuminated and challenged by the biblical image of Jesus. But our experience will also highlight and shape our interpretations of the ideas and images we find in the New Testament.

But what about the authority of the Bible, in relation to the authority of experience? What if professional judgment or the conviction of personal experience seem to conflict with what the New Testament Jesus calls us to do? Isn't a theology of Spirit simply a way of making a virtue of compromise?

A theology of conversation, by definition, means paying careful attention to both sources of authority. It seeks to make a virtue not of compromise, but of openness to the unlimited power and care of God for us in our diverse human contexts. It is when conflicts between professional goals and values and Christian goals and values arise, that theological engagement with others is most needed.

A theology of Spirit requires profound trust in the presence of God in the community of believers in two essential ways. First, it requires trust that when a professional brings his or her own theological conversation before the Christian community, God's presence will enable truth to emerge. While the New Testament remains the primary source against which we test our experience, interpretations of the ideas and images we find there *do* change as our experience changes. Some ideas and images gain increased or new meaning and prominence; others fade in importance. Note the rise of the historical-critical method and its impact on our biblical interpretation. Remember that the biblical call to mission gained in prominence among Mennonites as the nineteenth-century missionary movement developed. Consider that the changing interpretations of the biblical message about the role of women in the church occurred in the context of a larger, societal women's movement. Such changes are seen by some Christians as deviations from God's revealed truth; others understand them as God's prophetic voice for particular times. New interpretations may be either of these. But individuals who assume either one or the other from the outset deny the continued power of the Spirit of God among us.

For any individual or group within the church to hold to a fixed interpretation of the revelation of God in Jesus Christ without seeking to bring their theological conversation before others in the church is idolatrous. Such rigidity limits the power of God to act in new ways. We may find that we are among the blind, that in the end we have no ears to hear.

Second, theology of Spirit requires a trust in the support of others. When a professional brings an ethical dilemma before the primary community and concludes that the conflict between experience and the biblical call are irreconcilable, it requires confidence that God will move others to help him or her find sources of courage and practical aid in resigning from the professional situation or actively working to change it.

Often the choice for the professional is not limited to stark compromise or withdrawal. The burden of the Christian community is to help that person find creative ways of maximizing as many of the values at stake as possible. In response to my teaching dilemma at Melrose my congregation might have ideas about how to push the system into finding alternative educational environments for the problem students. Then I could have worked

---

Self in Conflict

By Joanna Johnson

I am an administrator of a human service organization that provides community based care for retarded persons who are leaving state hospitals. As a professional in the mental health field, I often feel an internal conflict between what I call my "Brethren" self and my "professional" self. I was raised with Anabaptist values in the Church of the Brethren. I was taught to be passive, to listen to the Spirit, to wait and receive, to be wise as a serpent and as innocent as a dove. I learned that I should not manipulate, manage, or "own" the world, since I was "in" but not "of" it. I grew up believing that it was wrong to be aggressive and that it always pays to turn the other cheek as set forth in the Sermon on the Mount. I learned to be hesitant, humble, cooperative, not "too assertive," and never to be "pushy." This was the profile of my Brethren self. I still cherish that self but find it often in conflict with my "professional" self.

To survive and be successful as a professional, I need to be aggressive and assertive. As a manager of a large human service organization I realize that I am the world—I am part of the system. To act as though I'm not part of it erodes my effectiveness to make the system work. I have to be part of the gang to get the job done. Talkative and aggressive behavior pays off for me. I deliberately use manipulative techniques and pick the battles that I can win and go

more effectively with the rest of the class. Members of the congregation might even have volunteered to work with such students themselves, or have helped to fund alternative educational staff or programs.

Theology and Life in Conversation

Because a theology of Spirit emphasizes God's presence in the *process* of theological conversation, I cannot conclude with an outline of a definitive theology for professionals. Each of us must define our own living theologies within our primary and extended community of believers. I can, however, note four Christian ideas that have become alive for me in bringing my

---

after them. There are very pragmatic things that I need to accomplish and I often need the power of intimidating force to do them. If I want to improve life for the retarded adults in our system, I need to control the system and the people who run it.

Sometime ago I was supervising a house parent who was treating her retarded clients like they were less than human. She refused supervision and knew how to manipulate the system so well that she had managed to eliminate three of her previous supervisors. I was at war with her. She threatened me physically. She wanted to "break" me and "destroy" me. It took all of the personal and professional clout and determination that I could muster

to fire her. I had to carefully protect our organization and myself legally in the process.

And so I frequently find my "Brethren" and "professional" selves in conflict. In my work, I often find the image of Jesus cleansing the temple more appealing than the Sermon on the Mount. And yet it's because of my "Brethren" self that I'm here working in an organization that helps mentally retarded adults. The values of servanthood led me here but they aren't always effective in accomplishing servanthood. In other words I often must be a manipulative master to be a servant of the retarded.

own professional experience into theological conversation. My experience has given new depths to the following Christian affirmations; the affirmations have challenged aspects of my professional life.

First of all, a living theology for me must be one that understands the ambiguities of professional power. Such a theology recognizes not only the dangers of human power but also the creative gift it is. Our images must include not only the nonresistant Jesus on the cross and the refusal of Jesus to accept the use of force in the temptation accounts, but also images of Jesus and the money changers and Jesus' healing on the Sabbath.

A theology that understands these ambiguities neither unduly condemns nor reveres power initially, but examines particular cases to see whether such power is being used responsibly to love God and others. Such a theology can recognize without apology the fundamental inequality between client and professional. It can affirm the need for exclusive professional standards so that clients are protected from incompetent advice. At the same time, it notes the vulnerability of clients. This imbalance places special responsibility on professionals to guard their use of power. Paternalism is a strong temptation and should be constantly limited by a professional's commitment to maximize the decision-making role of the client.

Second, a living theology for me recognizes that God gives varied gifts, tasks, and understanding to different people but values our best contributions equally. Such a theology affirms the validity of professional specialization but does not make the corresponding value judgment that in the service of God and others professional work is more meritorious than lay work. This claim will affect a common professional attitude—hostility on the part of professionals toward lay people who do not share their professional standards of judgment. Professionals who take the idea of varied gifts but equal value seriously are able to step far enough outside their own profession to recognize the value of nonprofessional judgment in some cases, especially on moral issues relating to the profession. Such a commitment can help them remain critical of their own tendency to disrespect clients who do not agree with the professional's view of the world. The understanding of varied gifts should also remind us that not every professional needs to "love" a client in the same way. A brilliant lecturer may not need to handle student conferences well; a highly skilled surgeon need not have an outstanding bedside manner.

This view has implications for professional autonomy as well. While professionals are reluctant to delegate any power to others, a Christian professional committed to a theology of varied gifts can be more open to sharing power. While some physicians, for example, might resent the increasing role of nurses and midwives in primary health care and experience this as role deprivation, the Christian professional might interpret such personal role loss as the positive empowerment of others for the sake of offering more adequate total care for clients.

Third, a living theology for me includes a deep commitment to monotheism. A profession is never fully autonomous. Its most basic assumptions are limited by loyalty to God.

I know something about the process of becoming socialized into the academic profession. The pressures to succeed in a competitive job market, the shaping of one's goals and identity, the qualities one is encouraged to develop to make it as "good student" all lead one to use one's power for professional ends. There is no thought to evaluating how all this relates to one's ultimate commitment to love God and serve others.

While professional commitments need not conflict with loyalty to God, there are numerous times when the struggle to succeed professionally requires the sacrifice of family relations or encourages irresponsible spending to meet social expectations. Protesting unjust policies or exposing another professional's failure to live up to professional ethical standards may jeopardize one's job and/or reputation.

Celebrating monotheism can help keep numerous and conflicting values and commitments in perspective. In some cases acting out one's loyalty to God may mean that one will be asked to leave or will want to leave a professional situation altogether. Questions of serious structural injustice, for example, challenge a profession at its core.

Finally, a living theology for me sees the role of the church as essential. This substantive theological claim—that God's spirit is most clearly revealed in Christian community—returns us once again to the *process* of doing theology. Persistent and serious involvement with a primary and, if possible, extended community of believers can have enormous significance for providing guidance in sorting through the ambiguities of professional power. Engagement with a small group of believers is a concrete symbol of one's loyalty to God above the profession and a visible affirmation of one's acceptance of a theology of varied gifts of equal value. Life in the church serves as a tangible counterbalance to the powerful role of the professional community in one's self-definition and decision-making. A distinctively Anabaptist-Mennonite church will keep issues of pacifism, simplicity, church-state loyalty, voluntary membership, and so on, clearly in focus. But it will be the community's openness to the unfolding Spirit of God in their midst, the courage to engage in critical theological conversation, and the commitment to converse in spite of theological, professional, sexual, racial, or class differences that primarily marks them as God's children.

The church as the setting for the unfolding of God's spirit has relevance for the "stuff" of professional life, if we choose to make it so. The community will have no automatic answers to the questions like those Melrose raised for me. But it can provide a spiritual and intellectual context outside of the professional world where we might find new insights about the meaning of God and human life and new ways of seeing our particular experience. Corporate support and challenge can nurture a joint search for creative alternatives that remain as faithful as possible to Anabaptist-Mennonite values. It can also provide space for grieving when no alternatives but tragedy seem possible. The way for professionals, as well as for other Christians, might be narrow, but it may twist and turn in surprising directions.

CHAPTER TWENTY-ONE

Who Are
My People?

By Al Dueck

No One an Island

No one lives in isolation. My values are not only a product of my personal decisions. My identity is not simply a result of introspection. My world-view is more than the sum of my unique history. My career is more than my personal achievement. The assumption that the individual is the starting and stopping point for developing and understanding values, identity, vision, and work reflects the priority we give to the individual over community. Consequently we are often blind to the groups that influence us and we underestimate their power.

I assume that the individual *always* exists in a community and culture and is part of a "people." It is impossible to say "I" without at the same time saying "we." We are all members of communities that have a vision of how life should be lived. From the history of such a group we derive significant models, a unique vocabulary, and a sense of identity and belonging. And one's primary community (or network of significant other people) values some occupations over others and implicitly sets an acceptable standard of performance for them. The group we call our "people" nurtures us into meaning and direction. Thus the issue becomes not *whether* I have a people, but *who* are my people?

Two Communities

As Mennonites continue to move from villages to cities, professional and occupational groups become a more attractive "people" than the church community. It is the professional community that provides a new sense of identity in the modern culture. It is here that one obtains self-fulfillment. Professional colleagues become one's primary people—the significant others whose opinions matter.

The response of the church to the process of professionalization has varied from disinterest and preoccupation with its own programs to identification with a professional mentality in its way of being the church. A more faithful response is necessary.

The professional community socializes its members into its own perspective in a variety of ways. First, upon entering a

---

Does Faith Make a Difference?

By LeRoy S. Troyer

As a young boy, I thought that to serve God and to be respected in the Christian community I had to be a minister, a missionary, or work in a church agency. I feel differently now. But questions remain. Does one's faith make a difference in one's profession or work?

Early on I decided I wanted to allow the church, both our local congregation and the larger community, to form and shape my identity and practice. I did my thesis research at the University of Notre Dame in land planning, land use, and housing, with a special emphasis on preserving natural resources. Part of it involved designing a new community located in less productive agricultural land.

After graduating and opening my practice, I became active in architectural, professional, and local community organizations. I wanted to be accepted by my professional peers, learn the language they spoke, and establish a style for my practice. But after a few years, I began to realize that the church community was contributing more to my happiness and well-being, and challenging me more than any professional, community, or government organization. They all seemed to establish minimum

profession, graduate training provides contemporary role models in professors; reading lists indicate which people are worth listening to; and fellow students form a core of people with whom one can compare one's values and competencies. Licensure signals that one is legitimated by society and fosters professional identity by defining acceptable roles and standards of excellence.

Second, finding a rich network of friends with similar interests, concerns, and priorities reinforces the development of one's professional values and goals. The professional community displays its heroes for imitation and heralds its fund of folk wisdom and information. Associating with colleagues and immersing oneself in the subject matter of the discipline gives one a new language to describe reality, and a new way of defining and resolving problems.

---

standards, while the church worked toward ideal or optimum standards.

There were some areas of my practice that were difficult to relate to our local church community. Meanwhile, I learned of Mennonite Industry and Business Associates; there I found companionship with the larger brotherhood and church community. Also, our former pastor, Elvin Stoltzfus, encouraged me to work with and assist the Mennonite Board of Congregational Ministries on "meetinghouse" architecture.

It is dangerous for any society to give "professionals" freedom and control without accountability. Basic values, standards of excellence, and needs are defined by the client (community) with the architect acting only as a facilitator. Whenever possible, I try to identify and gather a team of specialists from various disciplines to address or solve special design needs of people. I feel more comfortable when the client and users of the physically built environment actively participate in the planning and design process.

I wanted to serve our local community and churches, so I started contributing some of my time and services. This was not always ef-

And third, the more organized and integrated the professional community, the greater are the expectations it makes of its members. If a professional group has a long history of status, or if it is presently fighting for a rung in the ladder of occupations, it tends to be more exacting in its demands for conformity to its behavioral standards and ideology. Consequently, one cannot assume that the professional community is a neutral community. Uncritical acceptance of the professional community as the context of one's work is to buy its frame of reference, people, values, and world-view as one's own.

To say that I am a Christian, however, is to accept another community where Yahweh is acknowledged as Creator and Jesus as Savior and Lord. When the church is faithful to this confession it relativizes all other communities. The vision of

---

fective, at times even misdirected, and I became frustrated after giving many hours a week while at the same time keeping my practice alive. Our pastor suggested that I might work with our church-wide agencies. As a professional, I can provide several weeks of volunteer service each year to the larger church community now, rather than waiting until I retire. As a result of a meeting arranged by Elvin Stoltzfus with the Mennonite Board of Congregational Ministries staff, I am now part of a team including a church historian, theologian, and educator, who conduct workshops on meetinghouse architecture. Since I work with a wide variety of people, I learned that many nonprofessionals also have good, creative ideas and workable solutions!

How does my faith specifically affect my profession? For me, the stewardship of our natural resources has always been a part of my practice. I work at this in the following ways:

- Planning new land use instead of the "broad acres" approach of the post-World War II suburban sprawls.
- Recycling, restoring, and adapting existing older buildings.
- Retrofitting both older and modern buildings for energy conservation and fuel cost efficiency.
- Using energy conscious designs for new buildings.
- Forming a new entity, Lead Group Incorporated, to provide a service of program development, life cycle costing, and construction management for facilities. Since the operating costs of buildings are often two to five

God's kingdom as set forth by Jesus in the Sermon on the Mount is then the starting point for values. God's people are to be characterized by love, servanthood, forgiveness, humility, peace, and joy. Members who covenant together to incarnate these kingdom values and who call each other to greater faithfulness and obedience make the church a primary community. It is in the context of this covenant community that the individual derives a sense of identity. It is an identity that is based on a new memory, the memory of God's faithfulness to his people throughout history. Individuals in that history who exemplified their faithfulness as disciples of Jesus become the primary heroes and models. The fellowship of believers creates a place one can call home.

But fellowship also means accountability to the larger church in decision-making. The New Testament church was inte-

---

times more over the life of the building than the initial building cost, we need to carefully plan before we build.

• Strongly encouraging churches to consider multi-use and better utilization of their meetinghouses. This often results in building less square footage, remodeling existing buildings, or not building at all, with the better use of existing facilities.

• Developing new ideas for energy conservation. Three years ago, I designed a cooling system for a restaurant that uses the earth's natural temperature for cooling in the summer and tempering the cold makeup air in winter. Now the Associated Mennonite Biblical Seminaries, in Elkhart, Indiana, is using this method to cool their offices at approximately 10 percent of normal air conditioning energy usage.

• Promoting an awareness of our diminishing resources by giving lectures to high school and college students and service clubs on energy conservation and stewardship of land use.

After six years of practicing architecture and after much thought and planning, I established a professional partnership and invited associates to join the partnership. All are invited into the partnership based on their abilities and experience with the firm. Since they are young, with limited financial resources and with young, growing families, they do not need to buy into the firm. However, the firm's financial growth is shared equally among all the partners. This allows the partners to receive the benefits of their own labor and develop their own equity in the partnership.

grally involved in the discernment of gifts and in their most appropriate use and application. Moreover, when the church is the context of ethical decision-making, ethical dilemmas are examined together. Then the church becomes an alternative context to one's professional community for evaluation of and critical reflection on professional work.

Who then are my people? The profession or the people of God? For the person who calls Jesus, Lord, there is no question; it is the people of God. But what does that mean? What are the implications for the *professional* who wishes to make the churchly community his or her reference point? What are the consequences for a *church* which seeks to provide a home for professionals?

Aptitude Tests in the Church

The church is involved in the affirmation of abilities. The church is a place where abilities can be tested. In the New Testament church this involved the discernment of gifts and the approval of a specific task by the laying on of hands.

Unfortunately the selection of a profession is increasingly left to the preferences, interests, or even whims of the individual. We urge young people to choose what seems good to them. Or we give vocational interest inventories so one can compare patterns of interests with professionals already on the job market.

But the fact that my experiences have produced a set of abilities that match that of an engineer, lawyer, or teacher is hardly sufficient reason to enter those professions. Such a process takes the types of occupations available in our society as the only given options. But some work may be inappropriate for Christians and some work more consistent with the needs of society as perceived by the church. Is the need for airline stewardesses as pressing as the need for nurses in Sudan? How would we counsel a young person to choose between being a psychologist or a pastor?

The task of the church then is to develop a sense of priorities in service to assist in the discernment of abilities. Abdication of this responsibility by the church reinforces the notion that selecting one's occupation is simply a matter of individual choice.

I Pledge Allegiance to . . .

When the professions demand loyalty, the church calls for conversion. Either because of its structure or because of its vision, the professional community tends to demand exclusive loyalty. This call for loyalty may depend on the length of the profession's history; it may be a defensive posture toward other professions; or it may be the result of motivation on the part of the individual professional. When one's work becomes the center of one's existence, the church calls for a radical transformation of allegiance. One can be committed to only *one* normative community.

My own training is in psychology. While in graduate school I wanted very much to enter the community of professional psychologists. I wanted to speak their language and master the subject matter. I wanted their status and their privilege. Their definition of excellence became my definition of excellence. I assumed that my witness as a Christian was dependent upon exceeding the professional standards of my colleagues. Needless to say, my commitment to the church waned and the time for my family dwindled. It was the faithfulness and love of a small Mennonite Brethren church that kept before me an alternative vision of discipleship. It resulted in a conversion, a change of loyalty from the professional community to that of the kingdom of God. I stopped seeing myself as one who was called to be a psychologist. Rather I was called simply to be a member of the God-movement. Gradually I wanted to be seen least of all as a psychologist and most of all as a brother. As I taught at a church-related college, I wanted the church rather than my professional discipline to shape the substance of my vision for life. I am embarrassed at how similar my courses were initially to the standard psychology courses offered at any public university. My commitment to the kingdom has resulted in some radical surgery in my courses. If one has developed a high level of professional commitment, being willing to make the kingdom of God primary will require a transformation of one's loyalties.

The Church as a Yardstick

The vision of the church provides a basis for critiquing the professions. Because we have too glibly blessed the profession with the notion of "calling," we must reflect critically on the role of professions in our society. Our criteria for evaluation must be consistent with the Christian community's vision.

Our age has been characterized as "the age of the disabling professions." The experts have taken control, adjudicated needs, nurtured dependence, and sapped resources. Meanwhile, lay persons have lost their ability to think and act for themselves. Through institutionalized power, a presumably esoteric body of knowledge, and a specialized language, the professional emerges as the new high priest of modern culture. He or she decides who shall be healed, when, and for how much. Not surprisingly, a group of people emerge with the label of "clients."

To fairly critique professions we must also critique the society which provides a home for them. First, professions emerge only in well developed societies. Both the nature and demands of such societies permit professions to flourish. A highly rational, technological society needs problem-oriented experts who can experiment with different methods, systematize procedures, and formalize regulations. The professional becomes a technician. Moreover, living in complex societies often results in individual disorientation. The tension, anxiety, and conflict of a highly competitive, work-oriented, and status-seeking society results in psychological casualties. The professions provide the psychic and physical healers, planners, and controllers.

Second, a particular culture's nature influences the form and content of professional service. It should come as no surprise that a pragmatic, market-oriented, bureaucratic society should sometimes produce professionals who worship technique, sacrifice service for fees, and idolize efficiency and routinization. Also, professions draw their wisdom and values from the surrounding culture. I am constantly amazed at the similarity of values between mental health professionals and our culture: individualism, growth, intimacy, and wholeness. The professions then are integrally related to our values and beliefs.

To the extent that the church has a unique vision and is not simply an extension of society, it will experience tension with the professional perspective. The dehumanization of some welfare institutions stands in contrast to the sanctity which Christianity gives to individual life. Personal and social healing cannot happen simply through intimacy of relationships or the manipulation of rewards. Renewal of the people of God is a consequence of God's faithfulness and comes as a result of the love and care experienced in the midst of God's people.

Our immediate reaction to criticism is to be on guard. If the professional community is my only community, I will inevitably be defensive. Such criticism, however, is the preparatory step to integration.

Creative Professionals

The vision of the historic Christian community is the basis for the development of creative, alternative forms of service. There need be no conflict between the professions and Christianity if there is continuity between the values of the profession and the kingdom. After all, the professions emerged in a context where Judeo-Christian values were espoused. However, the life and practice of the kingdom must motivate one's professional activity. Here are some examples of professionals I know, who, in my opinion, have done just that:

- the North American medical doctor who is able to leave home to serve in Cambodia, who attempts to treat a patient as a whole person, not simply a body or one of its parts;
- the architect who is committed to designing buildings and homes that reflect a concern about energy usage and land consumption;
- the lawyer who, because of God's particular love for the oppressed, chooses to work with the weak and helpless in tenant-landlord disputes;
- the counselor who doesn't simply reflect the emphasis on introspection

in our narcissistic culture but who calls for the development of
covenant relationships;

- the schoolteacher who teaches in a ghetto school but refuses to accept
  the prevalent assumption that since physical punishment is acceptable
  in lower social classes, it is the only way to maintain order and respect;
- the entrepreneur who considers profit-sharing as a way of creating
  community between employees and employers;
- the pastor who resists assuming responsibility for all programming and
  decision-making rather than sharing leadership functions;
- the college teacher who is less interested in producing marketable majors but focuses on faithful discipleship and models commitment to the
  church;
- the social worker who imitates Paul's desire to break down the walls
  between Jew and Greek by bringing together a victim of a crime and
  the offender in the hope of reconciliation.

The Buck Stops at Church

The church community is the locus of accountability.
Professions tend to assume independence and autonomy. They
develop a morality of their own. Members are expected to be accountable to the professional society over other groups. The
professional community has knowledge and a perspective on
certain issues that lay persons presumably cannot understand.
Hence, if the church presumes it has something to say it is often
perceived as meddling.

The Christian who takes the church as the community of
discernment is accountable to his or her brothers and sisters. As a
Christian, my functioning in a particular profession affects the
witness of the church to the human community.

Not only is the church the locus of accountability. It *is* quite
capable of responding to ethical matters once the issues are
explained. The problem of abortion and euthanasia for the
medical doctor must be examined with other Christians. The use
of chemicals and certain pesticides is not simply a personal matter to be decided by each farmer. Patient and client rights can be
discussed profitably by those on the receiving end of professional
services. Employer-employee relations can be examined to determine a Christian response in a legal dispute.

The church then is the center of accountability and discernment in ethical issues. It is not merely one more group in which the professional is a member. These are his or her people. To take that seriously means that one seeks to involve the church in the problems faced by professionals. The problem of one person in the church is a problem for all.

Optometrists for the Church's Vision

The professional can help the church to be faithful to its vision. Perhaps one of the reasons professionalism has become such a problem is because the church itself has bought into the professionalism mentality. Pastors who preach in the specialized jargon of theology are little different than professional psychologists who parade their vocabulary. The way we organize our church life at times differs little from the organizational charts of large bureaucracies. We have become as growth conscious as most financial organizations. When we assume that God is no larger than the perspective of our own community, we are as provincial as many professional groups. If there is little tolerance of diversity, we are like the professions themselves in demanding a conformity that destroys life in communities. A professional then can help the church reflect on its vision and practice so that it avoids the traps of professionalism.

Trained professionals can also assist the church in its tasks and in selecting those dimensions of culture that enable her to be more faithful. I have seen professionals who are sensitive to the vision of the church offer their skills in administration, counseling, education, music, building design and construction, legal aid, and medical help. The temptation for the professional will be to borrow uncritically from the knowledge of a discipline and thus unconsciously subvert the unique vision of the church.

In the relationship of the church to the professions, there is a place for each to critique the other, to quietly listen, to accept correction, to wrestle with problems, and to forgive errors. Conflict between church and profession is inevitable when the profession assumes absolute commitment or when the church presumes that its life completely reflects the kingdom of God.

CHAPTER TWENTY-TWO

What Makes Professional Service Christian?

By Ruth Hartzler Martin

Integrating Faith and Profession

Does Christian faith make one's professional service different from the service of a non-Christian? Many of Christ's teachings on attitudes and interpersonal relationships have been adopted by persons who do not call themselves Christian. As a result, many non-Christians provide loving and caring service that may not look much different than the service of Christians. This essay does not identify differences between the professional services of non-Christians and Christians, however; instead, it looks at some of the ways Christian professionals can apply the teachings of Christ to professional service.

Professional service cannot be labeled Christian or unchristian. Likewise, professions and vocations are not Christian. I think it is more precise to apply the adjective "Christian" to a person rather than to the effort of that person. We don't talk about the service of those embracing Islam or Buddhism as being Islamic or Buddhist service. But somehow we have come to think about Christian service as being different from secular service. The services of one who seeks to live out the teachings of Christ should reflect the attitudes and teachings of Christ.

In the work world specific tasks can be carried out in a variety of ways; perfunctorily, carelessly, carefully, or precisely. One can be cold, careless, disdainful, angry, pleasant, cheerful, concerned, loving, and caring.

We can hardly be Christian professionals unless we integrate the characteristics of Christ and the attitudes he taught into our professional service. The great amount of time and energy spent in professional service cannot be divorced from the "Christian" part of life.

There are biblical themes which speak to professional service. Christ stated that he came to serve, not to be served (Mark 10:45); thus a strong Anabaptist stance has been that our work should serve others. Paul instructed the Colossians that in whatever they do they should put their whole heart into it as if they were doing it for the Lord (Colossians 3:23). Christ also taught that his followers must leave self behind (Mark 8:34). The second greatest commandment (Matthew 22:39) stresses that we must love our neighbor as ourself. Other passages suggest that the variety of gifts—personal abilities—with which members are endowed are to be exercised and definitely used for the benefit of others. The golden rule (Matthew 7:12) teaches us to treat others in the way we want to be treated. And above all, we are to love God with all our heart, soul, and mind (Matthew 22:37).

Loving God and Professionalism

Most of us probably entered a profession to be a more effective Christian disciple. We saw our professional preparation as one way for God to work more fully through us. We may also have seen the profession as a means to the kind of lifestyle we wanted while at the same time contributing a genuine service. We may have sensed a calling to the profession we entered. Since the ideals of most professions are congruent with Christian faith, and since our motivation for entering a profession is for the most part wholesome, it is easy to assume that fervent professionalism is the highest form of Christian service.

Professions demand a great investment of time and energy from their members, and a high degree of commitment to their goals and ideals. This is true not only during the time of formal education, but continues as professionals need to maintain their competency. "Keeping up" requires a great deal of time reading professional literature, interacting with professional colleagues, attending professional meetings, conducting research, and sharing the findings of that research. Some of these activities may be included in our workday, but often much needs to be done on one's "own time." Failure to "keep up" supposedly brings about

---

Why I Taught Comp 101

By A. Grace Wenger

Ernie could dribble a ball across the court with grace and ease, but he fumbled through a simple writing assignment. Yet I saw intelligence and determination in the black eyes that watched me intently, I liked the smile that widened slowly across the handsome face as my explanation became clear, and I could only guess at the courage it took for a young man from an inner-city high school to enter college in surroundings as unfamiliar as a foreign country.

One hour of individualized instruction a week for one semester was all it took to help Ernie hold his own among classmates from well-run high schools in suburban communities. Each year I saw him walk taller and more proudly, and a few years later the smile flashed swiftly when Ernie told me he was beginning graduate study. Ernie didn't know it, but he helped me answer the question, "What difference does being a Christian make in the way I function as an English teacher?"

After twenty-two years of teaching in Mennonite high schools, where a teacher's freedom to share faith was appreciated, even expected, I had to ask myself how to express a faithful Christian witness as a professor in a state college. Certainly I had no plans to reserve the college auditorium and hold evangelistic services as a fundamentalist colleague had done some years earlier. It did not seem ethical to use a classroom lectern as a podium for Christian polemics, nor quite consistent with the Anabaptist position on separation of church and state. And the initial coolness of a colleague who later admitted to having roomed at the university with a Mennonite (from a branch of the church known for its evangelistic fervor) did not increase my confidence in "ten easy steps in soul-winning."

As I felt my way in the new situation, I began to understand that following Christ in servanthood would be an important part of my witness. Servanthood meant obsolescence and/or a reputation of incompetence.

Christ also demands a commitment of our total being to him. This includes the development and nurture of our individual relationship with God and commitment to our families and the members of the Christian community of which we are a part. Time and energy are needed for caring, sharing, listening,

---

voluntarily moving into the place of real need. Instead of competing to teach prestigious upper-level elective courses, a servant would joyfully teach the composition class required of all freshmen, a job that most large universities thrust upon student assistants. Instead of reading poetry with English majors who already loved it, a servant would share the excitement of literature with non-majors who thought they hated it.

Then along came Ernie. There were others too. An increasing number of Spanish-speaking, urban black, and foreign students were entering our institution. For those who lacked skill in standard English, admission often became a revolving door. I could not callously say (as did some professors), "Let them learn to write correct English before they come to college." It seemed equally irresponsible to give passing grades for substandard work. My experience with Ernie, and with Terri, Athena, Faraden, and others, had convinced me of the academic potential of nontraditional students. Here was an opportunity for real servanthood.

I took a leave of absence to learn how to teach English as a second language and as a second dialect, beginning with courses in linguistics, for my training had been in literature. After a year and several summers of study, I returned to teach a fundamentals of writing course designed for nontraditional students, as well as a special section of English composition for traditional students with writing problems. An influx of Vietnamese students began that year, and I never had to ask myself whether my service was worthwhile. Friends had warned me that my new schedule would bore me to death. But through the mysterious laws of the kingdom of servanthood, I recaptured (after more than a third of a century of teaching) something of the excitement of my first years in the classroom.

discipline, and teaching. Time for spiritual growth must be allocated just as conscientiously as for our professional growth. The competition for primary allegiance must be recognized when we think about our personal and professional values, our standards of conduct, and to whom we feel most accountable. We may need to review this matter with ourselves daily, weekly, or monthly to maintain the perspectives we want in life.

We must also question what level of professional competency is adequate and necessary. Can we be comfortable with reasonable but not mediocre effort? Do we really need a higher academic degree to provide the kind of service we do best?

I am not suggesting that Christian professionals should be incompetent professionals. Sweet smiles cannot substitute for professional competence, although people often do need love and empathic concern more than they need refined professional competence.

Overzealous professionals—even in the name of Christian service—may burn out. In fact it may be a particular problem for those who take seriously Christ's teaching that his followers must leave self behind. Whatever that teaching was trying to tell us, Christ's personal example involved time for personal renewal and refreshment. As Christian professionals we need to develop a healthy balance between being attuned to the hurts of others and renewing our own inner resources.

Christ's renewal times were often spent in the company of his disciples. Surely the closeness and interdependence which developed during their times together helped each disciple cope with distressing situations. Persons must *receive* caring if their abilities to care for others are to remain vital and meaningful. A balance of aloneness and intimate personal sharing with others is necessary for personal renewal and reflection.

Blurred Clients

It is easy for Christian professionals to lose their focus on the client, patient, or student and become preoccupied with their own performance, prestige, and professional concerns. The focus on personal and professional concerns instead of on client service is often fostered by competition among peers who want attention from superiors who grant raises, privileges, promotions, and commendations.

The heavy emphasis on evaluation of services can also shift the focus from the client, patient, or student to the professional providing the services. Providers of service sooner or later are evaluated by someone. The evaluators can be peers, clients, superiors in the organization, boards of directors, accrediting or regulating agencies, even the members of one's geographical community. Awards recognizing outstanding achievement are another kind of professional evaluation of one's abilities and accomplishments. The efforts required to "pass" all these evaluations may deprive clients of necessary care and attention.

As a Christian professional, I have a special calling to demonstrate attitudes which recognize the personal worth of those I serve, those in authority over me, my peers, those I supervise, advise, represent, and those whose service supports mine. To teach, serve, represent, or care for persons in an automated, calloused, depersonalized manner which fails to recognize their uniqueness as individuals is contrary to the way of Christ. Although Christ was confronted by crowds, he healed individuals, not crowds. In his one-to-one encounters there was always a personal concern for that individual's welfare and a recognition of the uniqueness of the special needs of that person.

We lump individuals together and think of them as welfare mothers, undergraduates, rowdy third-graders, the patients on east wing, my accounts, a bunch of neurotics, and my caseload. We seldom use such depersonalized labels when we have intimate knowledge of the individuals we serve.

The reasons for depersonalizing groups of people vary. Sometimes there is too little time to develop personal relationships with those we serve as in some clinic situations. In other cases, the clients may be a name on a list or a voice on the phone, as often happens in a social worker's or personnel director's office. Sometimes the physical needs of patients in a hospital demand so much attention that there is little energy to care about the person's emotional needs. Sometimes the large number of students in a classroom makes it impossible to know each one individually. Sometimes we find it hard to empathize with the needs of those we serve.

Professional Clout

The use of professional power is another area where the influence of Christ's teachings can make a difference. Professionals have, use, covet, and seek more power. Without power much good could not be accomplished. Power corrupts, however, when it deprives people of services, allows incompetent persons to practice, prevents persons from giving honest opinions, and when it dominates instead of collaborates. Christian professionals are responsible to use their power to provide services to people who need them, to prevent injuries by recommending competent professionals, to demonstrate collaboration instead of domination with other professionals (including male-female relationships), and to speak the truth with love when evaluating others' service. Christ used his power to provide healing, to teach people how to live, to help the powerless, and to free people from fear and personal burdens. He taught that those who wished to be great—that is, possess power—would have to become servants (Mark 10:43-44).

Collective bargaining is one example of the raw use of power in professional life which often cripples service and diverts attention away from the client, patient, or student. More and more professionals in the fields of health care, education, and social service are expected to participate in these labor activities. If fellow professionals are organized for collective bargaining, the Christian professional should investigate those processes and procedures so that an intelligent, informed decision can be made *before* a strike occurs.

Generally the real issues leading to strikes involve economic issues. Strikes bring losses to both the employee and the employer, to say nothing about the clients, patients, or students. Because strikes are a result of failure to agree on work-service matters, they tend to be expressions of anger, resentment, and mistrust. Relationships between management and the work force are frequently wounded during a strike. Such hurts often never heal or leave permanent scars at best.

But questions abound. Does positive participation in a strike in the hope of improving one's personal status justify an interruption of service to clients? What will happen to one's professional influence and reputation with peers and superiors if one does not participate in a strike? How is this likely to affect one's ability to provide service in the future within that setting? What is likely to happen to the confidence of clients, patients, and students in the services one offers? Will one's ability to provide services be enhanced or hindered by participating in a strike?

Good Pipes and Theories

Our overall attitude toward work reveals whether we are giving our service cheerfully as though it were a gift of love or whether it is given primarily in exchange for a nice paycheck. Is our professional service an offering of our special gifts to others who need them? Or do we serve primarily to enjoy the rewards of recognition, prestige, and power? Do we go the second mile by giving a few extra minutes when they're especially needed? Do we ungrudgingly give a good measure of service in return for the fees we charge or the salary we receive? Do we view the value of each person's work as expressed by this poster message:

> The society which scorns excellence in plumbing as a humble activity and tolerates shoddiness in philosophy because it is an exalted activity will have neither good plumbing nor good philosophy. Neither its pipes nor its theories will hold water.

Are we trustworthy, fair, and honest or do we grant ourselves special privileges which we deny to others? Are we professionally distant, formal, and correct or do we allow genuine love, spontaneous compassion, and authentic caring to fill our relationships with clients and other professionals?

As Christian professionals we have a mandate from Christ to express unconditional love, unmerited mercy, and caring concern to those we serve. Furthermore, our services can lead others to new understandings and offer them hope from despair and freedom from fear. We are freed from undue self-concern and enabled to focus on those we serve with personal, caring love. Without guilt we can take time out of hectic schedules for renewal and refreshment so that we can maintain our emotional and spiritual resources for loving service. Our faith allows us to offer our professional services as gifts to serve the needs of others. Lastly, we recognize the value and usefulness of power and the responsibility to use it carefully for the benefit of others as well as ourselves.

Caught in the Middle

By Rodney E. Houser

As a teacher in a rural-suburban high school in a conservative rural community, I never expected to become involved in a teachers' strike. But at a union meeting after a preschool workshop on September 2 a vote was taken to authorize a strike. I voted in favor because I thought our issues were legitimate and I didn't expect the strike to happen.

The next morning the phone rang at 6:00 a.m. and I was told, "We are on strike. Pickets report to your assigned locations. All others report to strike headquarters." I had decided not to picket nor to cross a picket line. Now I really didn't know what to do. A strike seemed like an unprofessional and demeaning thing. This was my home community and I didn't want to be seen on a picket line—I would have felt and looked silly there. Reluctantly I went to the strike headquarters. My good friends were out picketing and kept asking for more help. I considered going home to wait it out. Yet I hated to leave because I, too, felt strongly about the issues. So finally I went to a store, bought some lunch, and distributed it to the picketers. It was my way of encouraging them without standing on the line.

The union asked for volunteers to answer a community hot line and to set up coffee klatches with parents. I volunteered for both. I took the first call that came in on the hot line—a personal acquaintance who now was an angry parent. I described the teachers' side of the issues to her and for the first time I really felt okay about my involvement in the strike.

I organized a meeting with parents from the local Mennonite church. Their feelings about the strike were hostile. They felt the teachers weren't justified and would never be able to regain the respect of the students. I really felt caught between my colleagues and my friends in the church. Whose side was I on?

The meetings at the church were helpful. Although the parents did not support the teachers' position, they appreciated my personal dilemma and accepted me personally. Months later they said, "We hope we weren't too hard on you." At the beginning of these meetings I identified primarily with the teachers, but by the end I also felt more closely identified with my friends in the church.

As the strike continued, I felt more positive about it. The refusal of the school board to consider the issues we were raising was even more demeaning than the strike itself. It was an agonizing experience for me. It was painful for all the teachers, but their spirit was one of taking a necessary stand rather than one of vengeful retaliation. Some good things came out of it. Now the administration treats teachers with more respect and dignity. There are few permanent scars. Surprisingly, the students said very little about it, though one wore a shirt with the slogan "striking teachers have no class."

In light of the good things that came out of it, I think I would vote again to authorize a strike if the issues were similar. A Christian colleague said, "A strike is a non-violent way to act against an unjust school board." That's a way to cloak the whole issue in some good sounding Anabaptist language. The quote sounds a bit contrived and like an attempt to justify something that you're not completely sure about. I'm still ambivalent but I realize the strike is not the bottom of the professional totem pole. It doesn't hurt people and it forces conflicting groups to deal with their concerns. Although I don't prefer a strike, I have a new appreciation for the whole process.

CHAPTER TWENTY-THREE

Can I Be a Creative Subversive?

By Calvin W. Redekop

The Limits of Professionalism

According to folk wisdom, hindsight is always 20/20. I am not so sure that is always true; in fact it may be that we sometimes never fully understand why we do certain things. Thus I don't think I understand fully why I refused ordination when my professors in college and seminary tried to influence me in that direction. Was I calloused to the Spirit's wooing? I don't think so, for I experienced considerable mental anguish over that issue. At the time, my rationale was that "I can do more good as a lay Christian than as an ordained Christian." I still feel the same, and I answer in a similar vein when the question occasionally comes up. With growing *hindsight* I am beginning to think I was acting on a creative impulse which at the time I did not fully understand, but which, as I shall argue here, is central to the creative encounter of gospel and life.

Professionalization (that moving in one's behavior and attitudes toward a more specific social role) is at once a basic need of the individual and the society, as well as a serious hindrance and liability. The professions have provided personal expression and identity for the individual and cohesion and productivity for the society. Almost all social institutions have developed professions in order to maximize productivity, efficiency, direction, and orientation. Professions and professionalism are detrimental only when the financial costs are considerable and when the benefits are at the expense of human values and relationships. How does one know when professionalization has gone far enough that it requires subversion?

The counterproductivity of professions and professionalism is evident in almost every sphere of our lives: The Jeff-Vanderlou housing project in St. Louis, Missouri, was not even completed when it became clear that it would have to be dismantled, and indeed it was. City planners, politicians, designers, architects, builders, and developers did their "professional best," only to have it result in a grand fiasco. Or consider the artists, designers, engineers, planners, and admen who almost succeeded in bankrupting Chrysler Motor Corporation with "professionally" produced dinosaurs despite obvious indicators that energy restraints were imperative. (This does not excuse Chrysler management who can be accused of "professional management" rather than creative behavior.) Warfare is another more grisly example. The professional soldier can now kill the enemy, including helpless children, with such rationalized and sophisticated flair that he sees no blood. And of course, many people have known that if the professional soldiers had their say, all of our conflicts would have been solved long ago.

Four Dangers

First of all, professionalism can separate personal and professional ethics. In almost every sphere of social existence, the individual conscience, values, and purposes are subordinated to the organization or body with which one is affiliated. Thus Max Lerner (1975), trying to make sense of Watergate, said, "The worst thing that has happened to professionals has been the divorce between their professional and business life and their personal life. . . . The most glaring example of this dichotomy will be found in the professional mobster, who kills when he wants to dispose of competitors but is sentimental about his family."

Second, professional values and ethics are usually the lowest common denominator of the collective. Again, as Lerner (1975) says, this means that businessmen "have an ethic, but it is the wrong one. It is, to use the common business phrase, a 'bottom line' ethic, that of the bottom line profit figure in a quarterly or annual corporate statement." This cannot be the basis for a viable social ethic for, as Lerner says, "The bottom line is what counts, whatever the means used. It is the cancer of the professions." It is bad enough to separate personal from professional ethics, it is even more insidious to uncritically accept the ethics of the profession as one's own especially when they are "benignly immoral."

Third, commitment to the professional complex can alienate a person from his neighbor. In normal human relations, be they business or social, the encounter is direct, face-to-face, and personal. In a highly professionalized situation, persons become specialists and "cases." As Lerner (1975) describes it, "A case in point is the medical profession, which has become a cluster of highly technical specializations in which not only the patient gets lost but also the doctor." Professionalism often creates a veil between oneself and one's neighbor; what is especially manipulative is that the professional can pull the veil down as much as he or she desires, while the "patient" is helpless to do anything about it. No one can argue with an invoice; it is an indisputable fact.

Finally, a profession can become a surrogate church. It often becomes the basic source of beliefs, values, and attitudes of the individual, as well as the satisfier of emotional and relational needs. Lester Anderson (1974:16-17) describes the preparation for professionals in a candid way: "Socialization produces the autonomous professional who knows who he is, is committed to his profession, and is motivated to serve as a professional throughout his work career. Consequently the professional person through the socialization process achieves identity, autonomy, commitment, and motivation." There is hardly a way in which the total commitment of professionalism could be more accurately described. Because they are so economically and socially rewarding, the professions have a powerful way of consuming one's total commitment and even becoming one's ultimate "church."

The Necessity of Subversion

It should be obvious that these four problems should be strenuously combated, regardless of whether one is a Christian or not. A secular ethic does not condone separating professional

---

Prison Doctor

By Kenneth J. Brubaker

For the past several years, Dr. J. Kenneth Brubaker has been medical director at the Lancaster County Prison while maintaining suburban practice in a family health center. He reflected with the editors about why he became a prison doctor.

Some time ago one of my friends who is an attorney was contemplating working as a public defender. My reaction was, "Why would you ever want to defend guilty people?" That conversation whetted my appetite to learn more about our local prison system. I soon discovered that the medical care was poor and so our group of physicians decided to apply for the medical services contract with the prison and I was named medical director.

Prisons are hard places to work. The physicians who usually end up there can't make it in a regular practice or are just trying to earn a few extra bucks while starting a regular practice on the outside. So

often the physicians don't have a strong, long-term commitment to high quality health care. Besides, a jail is a hard place to work. The prisoners often have multiple problems—emotional, medical, social, and economical. Often they don't want to be helped. The offenders see the prison doctor as part of the whole system that's out to get them. There are malpractice and physical threats. Most of the prison employees don't know how to care—they have a punishment mentality. A prison is primarily concerned about security and everything else is far behind. It's a very authoritarian environment—and it forces you to relate to other people that way—with little feeling.

I guess I feel that part of my life and professional efforts should be devoted to serving the poor and needy even if they don't give warm fuzzies in return like suburban clients do. And I'm pleased with

from personal ethics, nor does it advocate the use of the professional veil resulting in social alienation. Note that even a self-designated atheist, Marx, condemned the alienation that industrialism perpetrated on laborers.

The Christian is constrained by Jesus' comprehensive ethic which does not allow anything to come between a person and his or her neighbor. It is possible that one of the most relevant in-

---

the progress we've made in a few years. Now the prison is almost up to the American Medical Association's standards. We have more and better trained nurses. We will soon have a full-time psychiatric nurse. There's been a major change in the attitude of the health care personnel. Prisoners no longer see us as part of the enemy and we've developed good relations with the prison administration. We have special diets available now and have a curtain in the examining room—that took two years.

When I started, there was no private area in our clinic. A prisoner would usually be stripped for examination in front of other prisoners, some female nurses, and a guard. It's a good example of how a prison system strips you of your dignity. Anyway, I tried to get a curtain so that the exams could be done in private. Prisons are oriented toward crisis and this wasn't a crisis and it took two years but now we have a little cur-

tain and a lot more dignity!

I've learned a lot about the injustice of our justice system. I realize now that some of the offenders aren't guilty and that many are in there because they weren't rich enough to pay bail. Although many aren't particularly attractive persons with all their problems, for the most part they are products of very bad environments over which they have limited control.

Prisoners are one of our biggest "hidden" groups in society. I dream now about alternatives to prison—new options for rehabilitation that will keep people out. I realize that one reason the prison can't change is the political realities on the street. The best way for a politician to get elected is to promise tougher and tighter prisons for criminals. That's a hard force to buck. I'm impressed with how little church people know about prisons and our penal system. I think it's urgent that the Christian community be informed.

terpretations of the Good Samaritan is to beware of the danger of professionalism becoming a barrier between humans. The priest and the Levite both hid behind their professional roles in ignoring their responsibilities to the neighbor. The Samaritan, responding to his neighbor in an open, natural, and compassionate way, was held up by Jesus as the Christian model of human relationships. A basic principle should be that any expression of a social role or status which interferes in the expression of love and compassion for one's neighbor is by definition unchristian and thereby evil. The priest and Levite could be considered professionals, and with ultimate irony, religious professionals. Thus the principle should include "any religious professionals." In fact, in a penetrating discussion of work and calling, Jacques Ellul (1974) makes the case as strongly as it can be put: A vocation "represents a total divorce between what society unceasingly asks of us and God's will. Service to God cannot be written into a profession." I begin therefore with the assumption that professions and professionalism can mitigate service in the kingdom of God. How then can we responsibly subvert the professions and professionalism?

Creative Subversion

Through the years, I have received increasing satisfaction in confusing people when it comes to classifying my own professional activities. Even though I was never ordained, I have managed to "preach" in many churches, although both my hearers and I have usually avoided calling my orations "sermons." (Whether my hearers refused to call them sermons because they made no sense is a matter to which I cannot speak, because I have been too embarrassed to ask.)

I would like to address the problems of professionalism with specific and actual experiences. I do this at the risk of appearing boastful; I share it as personal testimony and confession of how I have tried to be creative in my subversion of professionalism. An obvious way to make sure that personal and social morality are not separated is to refuse to work in professions where such a divorce is demanded. Many occupations and professions were automatically excluded for me, since I knew that they would demand incompatible behavior. But what of areas which are ambiguous, such as business? Early in my adult life, I excluded a business career because I felt the values and ethics in that sector could not be harmonized with the Christian way. I decided that education was a field where I could retain a unified personal and institutional ethic in education, but it is not easy.

The temptation to accept the "orthodox" position of empiricism with its evolutionary assumptions is strong in social science. To "move up" in this profession depends largely upon one's willingness to believe its "line." Realizing this meant that I needed to accept the fact that I would never become a "biggie" in professional sociology. So I have tried to be as productive and creative as I could within the limits of my values. The bulk of my writing and teaching has not been "orthodox," but hopefully it has made a contribution to a larger circle beyond professional sociologists. I am aware that it is not always possible to choose a job where one can harmonize the private and professional role, but the challenge to be creative remains.

Multiple Professions

The second problem of accepting the values and behaviors of professions as one's operating base is more subtle, and deals with a commitment to the profession itself. I began to venture into business after realizing that I could be involved, yet still retain personal integrity. I was surprised to learn that it was relatively easy for me not to buy into the "bottom line" ethic of business, with its values of "all that matters is profits," or the view that "the disparity between the managers and laborers is a reward for risk." Perhaps because I had developed at least two or three professional identities, my identity was not dependent on any single one. It allowed me the luxury of being a "stranger" who could dip in and out of a profession without being totally reliant upon the acceptance of any one professional community. So when I made "ridiculous" proposals about how businesses should be run, I was patronizingly regarded as "that crazy professor who means well" who is to be complimented for "trying to understand the business world." On the other hand, when I refused the "publish or perish" syndrome of the academic community, I was usually greeted with the quietly envious retort, "You can thumb your nose at the academic rat race, because you are independently wealthy." (The flattery was too sweet to correct them of their misperception of my financial status.)

Thus one of the ways to be creatively subversive of professionalism is to be involved in as many professions as possible. I am encountering increasing numbers of people who are discovering this approach to creative subversion. If this professional meandering is not possible, one can cultivate friendships with persons in other fields who can provide the corrective and provocative perspectives which give a better balance. Incidentally, these friendships often offer the entrance into other professions. Everyone can develop a hobby, one of the easiest, most pleasant, and rewarding ways to protect oneself from the imperialism of professionalism. In fact, many of us are developing new and counterprofessions out of our hobbies. Some of my friends have made a very creative travel service out of a hobby, and I have become a travel guide through our friendship.

Loving Neighbors

Keeping the profession from alienating you from your neighbor is a very difficult assignment. The very purpose of professionalism—effectiveness, efficiency, competency, exclusion of competitors, specialization, predictability, management of clients, and a host of others—works for the professional's own benefit.

I have always been grateful that medical doctors *are* competent, knowledgeable, and efficient, but the temptation to allow the professional elements to become self-serving is always great, no matter what one's field. One can creatively subvert this temptation by not being totally dependent financially, socially, or status wise on any one profession or activity. Having financial earnings outside the teaching profession keeps me relatively casual and nonchalant about my professional academic image. On the other hand, my financial, occupational, and social security in the academic world has allowed me to develop generous and nonmaterialistic attitudes toward business and employee colleagues.

Involvement in community causes is a great way to subvert professionalism, both in the role you play and in the images you shatter. I have been involved in the establishment of two credit unions. The purposes of many such community organizations are compassion for the neighbor, and this helps to mitigate the claims and images of other professional roles. I have been asked, "How can you support a credit union when you are also in business? Don't you know these are in direct conflict?" Such questions open the door for exchange and reconciliation of opposing ideologies, and provide opportunity to explain my own attempt to see life more holistically. I know medical doctors and lawyers who are involved in community affairs, demonstrating that it's possible to keep a profession from becoming an all-encompassing commitment which sees neighbors as beings to ignore or exploit.

God's Local Chapter

A profession can easily become a surrogate church, not by crassly praying to Henry Ford, paying tithes to the American Manufacturing Association, or singing from *Odes to Capitalism;* rather, it happens in the subtle ways by which one's basic worldview, social concern, and contribution are determined by the profession. How does one keep one's loyalties straight and focused on the central question as asked by Allen Howe (1972): "How am I an integral part of the local chapter of the Kingdom movement?"

One of the most exciting "tricks" I have discovered in frustrating the profession from usurping my deepest commitment is to bring the church into the profession. The separation of the holy and unholy is necessary, but very delicate, and the attempts often lead us into hopeless dualism. We are the citizens of two kingdoms, but they do intersect and interact.

So how can business or other professions be kept in the Christian context? In several business ventures we started by selecting persons or couples who had similar beliefs, ethics, and interests. Then we wrote "charters of purpose" which stated our organizations' basic objectives and procedures. In this way the solar companies with which I am associated were in a sense the economic and business "extensions" of the congregation and its goals. We meet on Sunday morning for worship, praise, and fellowship, and during the week we meet in board meetings as the same people doing the corporate work, with a more holistic understanding.

Another type of subversion is to involve ministers and other churchly types in secular and/or professional activities. This works two ways; it "educates" the clerics and it keeps the professionals on their own toes. This is not a sure-fire tactic, since clerics can sometimes professionalize their roles in a curious Catch 22 fashion. They can "bend over backwards" and become the uncritical promoters, not only to gain acceptance, but to express long repressed frustrations at being excluded from the councils of power. Thus professional self-hatred can surface even among the most ordained among us.

Conclusion

It could be argued that a creative subversion of the professional structure is acting irresponsibly and contributing to social disorganization, even anarchism. The Christian, however, cannot be accused of anarchism because he has a vision or image of the society he is hoping to achieve—the kingdom of God. (And I suspect Plato would buy the vision of the kingdom of God, even if philosophers were not to be the kings!) Creative subversion of the professionalism which corrupts our society is a Christian responsibility.

With increasing satisfaction I like to confuse people when they ask, "How can you be in business when you hold a full academic job?" Or when they miss the connection between my dreaming of serving in a voluntary service program in Bolivia, my business obligations, and leading a tour group in Europe. I want my reply, either in word or behavior, to say, "It may not make a great deal of sense when considered from the treadmill point of view, but from another perspective, it's fun and reward-ing."

I feel confirmed in my view of subverting the professions be-cause I hear many friends through their example reminding me that Jesus said, "He who does not forsake all, and take up his cross and follow me, is not worthy of me." Professions and professionalism need not be a prison; they can be the framework from which we can expand and transform the world around us.

Perils of Professionalism:
A Summary

The sensitive professional is beleaguered with pitfalls. Seeing those traps is the beginning of change. Seeking ways to use one's best professional expertise, while skirting the snares, demands the collective wisdom of a faithful community.

For quick review we enumerate the hazards faced by a professional who is also a Christian. Here in distilled form are questions which, despite this book, remain in need of continual and creative solutions.

1. *Serving the Profession:* There is a widespread tendency for professionals to become so engulfed by their profession that they end up serving it rather than their clients, students, and patients. Is it possible to survive as a professional and not serve the profession? Are there ways to prevent a profession from dominating one's life and subverting genuine service to one's clientele?

2. *Twisting the Mythology:* Professional organizations and structures are inclined to use a generous sprinkling of humanitarian and Christian words while operating as greedy economic systems. Sometimes the "best interests" of the clients turn out to really mean protecting the best economic interests of the profession. How can professionals avoid the pitfalls of such distortion? In what ways can professionals speak the truth when the words of care and service are used as perverted window dressing?

3. *Believing the Mythology:* Professionals often find themselves believing and repeating the creed of their profession.

Most mythologies are self-serving and believable—they sound true at first. Common myths suggest that professionals care better, serve better, and are more dedicated than nonprofessionals. Each profession tends to view its solutions, practices, and perspectives as more holistic, more accurate, more complete, and more comprehensive than those of other professions. Is it useful to debunk the mythologies? How does one test the truth of such professional creeds? How does one develop defenses against gullibility?

4. *Separating from Others:* The professionalizing process based on specialization inherently pushes people apart—it places social distance between them. The extensive training separates professional from nonprofessional. The advanced specialization distances the professionals in one discipline from the professionals in another. The training, technical language, and diversity of experience pulls mother and daughter apart as well as professional and nonprofessional in the life of the church. Are there ways to bridge the gaps? Can the tendency toward separation and distance be reduced or even reversed?

5. *Breaking Up the Whole:* Another by-product of specialization is the tendency to divide people into fragments, to see their problem as a technical breakdown that can only be repaired by a specialist. Fragmentation limits our vision, constricts our caring, and narrows our service. It encourages professionals to be technical robots who fix parts, but who can't enjoy their clients or patients. Are there ways to be more than technicians who provide specialized fixes?

6. *Making Mystery:* Professions have a self-propelling fascination with mystery. Specialized language and ritualized procedures create a mysterious shroud over professional practice. This creation of awe, although not necessarily disabling, can be abused by the professional to create more social distance, to generate dependency, and to paralyze the critical attitude of clients. Are there creative ways to "translate" and "interpret" professional activity which minimize the peril of mystification?

7. *Guarding Secrets:* Secrets, when manufactured, must be

carefully guarded. Professions often spend a great deal of effort protecting their secrets from lay access. The professional turf is carefully drawn and fortified. What dangers arise if "secrets" are made readily available to the public? Are the monopolizing tendencies really beneficial for the public welfare and good?

8. *Manufacturing Need:* Professionals who are trained to serve the needy are in fact sometimes themselves the needy ones—in need of more clients. Through advertising, the prescription of unnecessary treatment, and the use of techniques without proven effectiveness it is possible for professionals to create a sense of need. How can individuals be certain that they are not manufacturing artificial need? How can professionals relate to their own profession or organization when it creates needs?

9. *Forgetting the Other Side:* After years of looking at the world through the lenses of one's own profession, the world can get quite lopsided. Professors easily forget the agony of taking an exam. Physicians forget the fear of pain and suffering. Counselors forget the stigma of needing emotional help. Henri Nouwen has suggested that those who are wounded are the best healers. What are some ways of straddling the fence, ways of becoming wounded healers, ways of becoming learning teachers?

10. *Refusing Review:* The more entrenched one becomes in the fortress of a profession, the easier it is to resist outside review, to believe that only one's like-minded fellow professionals are capable of evaluating and judging one's work. The temptation to believe in the myth of the "stupid and incompetent layperson" is strong. Are there creative modes of evaluation that go beyond critical nit-picking to joint efforts of reflection, review, and change by laypersons and professionals?

11. *Replacing the Church:* The church, as the primary source of values, significant others, standards of conduct, and ethical direction can easily be replaced by professional involvement. The profession as a surrogate church can quickly assert itself as the chief reservoir of values, friends, meaning, and purpose. The local church can easily become irrelevant and impotent in the life of a professional. Are there ways that the church can

effectively function as the primary community of discernment for professionals? Is it really feasible, for instance, to expect a local church to address the complicated ethical questions which a surgeon might face?

12. *Abusing Power:* Professionals have the power to define need, prescribe treatment, conduct therapy, and evaluate their own work. The mystery and aura of sophisticated technique and expertise can render a client vulnerable and powerless. Decisions may be imposed on the client in an intimidating fashion that "forces" the person to say "yes." Full information can easily be withheld. False impressions can quickly be created. The client may be presented with a very limited range of choice options. Professionals can easily assume that they always know what's best and manipulate situations and information to impose their preference.

Bibliography

Abbot, Andrew
    1981 "Status and Status Strain in the Professions." *The American Journal of Sociology.* 86:819-835.

Abrahamson, Mark
    1967 *The Professionals in the Organization.* New York: Rand McNally.

Albee, George W.
    1959 *Mental Health Power Needs.* New York: Basic Books.

Albee, George W.
    1969 "The Miracle of the Loaves and Fishes: Nonprofessionals for Everyone." Address to the National Association of Social Workers Leadership Training Program. May 1969; Chicago, Ill.

Anderson, Lester G.
    1974 *Trends in Education for the Professions.* Washington, D.C.: American Association of Higher Education.

Bledstein, Burton J.
    1976 *The Culture of Professionalism: The Middle Class and Development of Higher Education in America.* New York: W. W. Norton, esp. Ch. 3.

Brofenbrenner, Urie
    1973 "Who Cares for America's Children?" in *The Future of the Family.* Louise Kapp Howe, ed., New York: Simon & Schuster.

Burrow, James G.
    1977 *Organized Medicine in the Progressive Era: The Move Toward Monopoly.* Baltimore: Johns Hopkins University Press.

California Senate
    1953 Senate Interim Committee on Nurse Problems. *Final Report to the Legislature.* Sacramento, California State Printing Office.

1957a *Appendix to the Journal of the Senate.* Vol. II. Sacramento: California State Printing Office.

1957b Senate Interim Committee on the Treatment of Mental Illness. *Fourth Partial Report: A Suggested Training Program to Meet the Shortage of Psychiatric Personnel.* Sacramento; California State Printing Office.

1959 *Journal of the Senate.* Sacramento; California State Printing Office.

Daniels, Arlene Kaplan
   1974 "The Notion of Appropriate Professional Conduct: An Exercise in the Sociology of Sociology." *The American Sociologist,* November: 212-217.

Doudna, Christine
   1980 "Women at the Top," in *The New York Times Magazine,* November 30, pp. 54-120.

Dueck, Al
   1977 "On Becoming a Ph.D." Unpublished chapel address at Tabor College. October; Tabor, Kan.

Dueck, Al and Michael Regier
   "The Christian a Professional Psychologist?" Unpublished paper available from the authors.

Ellul, Jacques
   1974 "Work and Calling" in *Callings.* J. Y. Halloway and W. D. Campbell, eds. New York: Paulist Press.

   1970 *The Meaning of the City.* Grand Rapids: Eerdmans.

   1964 *The Technological Society.* New York: Knopf.

   1951 *The Presence of the Kingdom.* New York: Seabury Press.

Eisenberg, Richard
   1980 "How Employers Can Help," in *Money,* Vol. 9, No. 11, November, pp. 89-92.

Eisenstadt, Samuel N.
   1966 *Modernization: Protest and Change.* Englewood Cliffs, N. J.: Prentice-Hall, esp. ch. 1.

Etzioni, Amitai, ed.
  1969 *The Semi-Professions and their Organization.* New York: The Free Press.

Freidson, Eliot
  1970 *Profession of Medicine.* New York: Dodd, Mead & Co.

  1973 *The Professions and Their Prospects.* Beverly Hills, Calif.: Sage Publications.

  1975 *Doctoring Together: A Study of Professional Social Control.* New York: Elsevier, Inc.

  1977 "The Futures of Professionalization" in *Health and the Division of Labor.* M. Stacey, et al., eds., pp. 14-38, London: Croom Helm.

Gerstl, Joel and Glenn Jacobs, ed.
  1976 *Professions for the People: The Politics of Skill.* New York: Schenkman Publishing Co.

Glasse, James D.
  1968 *Profession: Minister.* Nashville: Abingdon.

Goode, William
  1957 "Community Within a Community: The Professions." *American Sociological Review.* 22:194-200.

Gross, Ronald and Paul Osterman
  1972 *The New Professionals.* New York: Simon & Schuster.

Harrison, Paul M.
  1959 *Authority and Power in the Free Church Tradition: A Social Case Study of the American Baptist Convention.* Princeton, New Jersey: Princeton University Press.

Herron, Willis
  1975 "Further Thoughts on Psychotherapy Deprofessionalization." *Journal of Humanistic Psychology,* 15:65-73.

Hofferth, Sandra L. and Moore, Kristina A.
  1979 "Women's Employment and Marriage," in *The Subtle Revolution; Women at Work,* Ralph E. Smith, ed., Washington, D.C.: The Urban Institute.

Howe, Allen
   1972 "Christian Vocation and the Kingdom Movement." Unpublished
        paper, Goshen College, convocation address.

Hughes, Everett Cherrington
   1958 *Men and Their Work,* Glencoe, Ill.: The Free Press.

Illich, Ivan
   1977 *Disabling Professions.* London: Marion Boyers.

   1980 *Toward a History of Needs.* New York: Bantam Books.

Jackson, J. A.
   1970 *Professions and Professionalization.* London: Cambridge University
        Press.

Jarvis, Peter
   1975 "The Parish Ministry: Semi-Profession." *The Sociological Review.*
        23:911-922.

Johnson, Terence J.
   1979 *Professions and Power.* London: Macmillan.

Kadushin, Charles
   1962 "Social Distance Between Client and Professional" in *American
        Journal of Sociology.* LXVII:5 March.

Kaufman, Gordon D.
   1979 *Nonresistance and Responsibility and Other Mennonite Essays.* Newton,
        Kan.: Faith & Life Press.

Krall, Ruth E.
   1971 *An Investigation of the Evolutionary Processes Involved in the Enactment
        of a Mandatory Licensure Statute for Psychiatric Technician in
        California.* Cincinnati, Ohio. The Graduate School of the University of
        Cincinnati.

Kraus, C. Norman
   1977 "The Christian Professional: Some Dangers and Opportunities,"
        Gospel Herald 70 (August 30, 1977). 650-652.

Khleif, Bud B.
   1975 "Professionalization of School Superintendents: A Sociological Study
        of an Elite Program." *Human Organization,* 34:301-308.

Langway, Lynn
1980 "The Superwoman Squeeze," in *Newsweek*, May 19, 1980, pp. 72-79.

Lieberman, Jethro K.
1970 *The Tyranny of the Experts*. New York: Walker & Co.

Larson, Magali Sarfatti
1977 *The Rise of Professionalism: A Sociological Analysis*. Berkeley: University of California Press.

Lerner, Max
1975 "The Shame of the Professions." *Saturday Review*. November 1.

Lubove, Roy
1965 *The Professional Altruist: The Emergence of Social Work as a Career 1880-1930*, New York: Athenum Press.

Lynn, Kenneth S. and the eds. of *Daedalus*
1965 *The Professions in America*. Boston: Houghton Mifflin.

May, William
1975 "Code, Covenant, Contract or Philanthropy." Hastings Center Report, Vol. 5, No. 6, December.

McKinlay, John B.
1973 "On the Professional Regulation of Change" in *The Professions and Social Change*, ed. by P. Halmos. Sociological Review Monograph No. 20, Washington, D.C.: American Sociological Association.

McKnight, John
1977 "Professionalized Service and Disabling Help" in *Disabling Professions*, I. Illich, ed. London: Marion Boyars.

Mennonite Student Services
1978 *Professionalism: Faith, Ethics, and Christian Identity*. Printed papers of a conference held in Philadelphia, Pa., March 1978. Available through Mennonite Board of Missions, Box 370, Elkhart, IN 46514.

1978 *Prophetic Vision Applied to One's Academic Discipline*. Printed papers from the 1978 Mennonite Graduate Seminar available through Mennonite Board of Missions, Box 370, Elkhart, IN 46514.

1979 *Conflict in the World of Professions*. Printed papers of a conference held in New York in February 1979. Available through Mennonite Board of Missions, Box 370, Elkhart, IN 46514.

Moltmann, Jürgen
   1978 "Diakonia in the Powers of the Holy Spirit." *Catalyst: A Resource for Christian Leaders.* (XLL) Waco, Tex.: Word.

Neufeld, Vernon H.
   1979 "A Call to Examine Human Services," "Methods and Motives in Serving," and "Kingdom Work and Human Services," *Mennonite Weekly Review.* July 12, 19, 26.

Nouwen, Henry J. M.
   1966 *Reaching Out.* Garden City, New York: Doubleday.

   1972 *The Wounded Healer: Ministry in Contemporary Society.* Garden City, New York: Doubleday.

Parsons, Talcott
   1939 "The Professions and Social Structure." *Social Forces.* 17:457-67.

Pavalko, Ronald M.
   1971 *Sociology of Occupations and Professions.* Itasca, Ill.: F. E. Peacock Publishers.

Physician's Daughter
   1975 "Letter to Dad," *Physician's Management.* October, pp. 25-27.

Raid, Howard
   1979 "Professionalism: The Last Refuge of a Scoundrel," "Professionals: The New Monopolists," and "Professionals: The New Community," *Mennonite Weekly Review,* September 20, 27; October 4.

Reese, Boyd
   1979 "Within or Outside the System: An Anabaptist Perspective," in *Conflict in the World of Professions.* Elkhart, Ind.: Mennonite Student and Young Adult Services.

Ritzer, George
   1975 "Professionalization, Bureaucratization and Rationalization: The Views of Max Weber." *Social Forces,* 53:627-34.

Runde, Robert
   1980 "How to Make the Most of Two Incomes," in *Money,* Vol. 9, No. 11, November, 1980, pp. 52-54.

Saint Exupery
   1943 *The Little Prince.* Paraphrase of an adult fairy tale cited in "Some Dy-
        namics of Medical Marriages," by Sarah Nelson. *Journal of the Royal
        College of General Practicioners,* October 1978.

Scott, Donald M.
   1978 *From Office to Profession: The New England Ministry, 1750-1850.*
        Philadelphia, Pa.: University of Pennsylvania Press, esp. chs. 4, 7, 9.

Seldon, William K.
   1968 "The Development of Professionalism in the Allied Health Field."
        Journal of American Medical Association. 206:1545-1547.

Steinzor, Bernard
   1967 *The Healing Partnership.* New York: Harper.

Trocmé, André
   1973 *Jesus and the Nonviolent Revolution.* Scottdale, Pa.: Herald Press.

Trunzo, Candace E.
   1980 "Mixing Children and Jobs," in *Money,* Vol. 9, No. 11, November
        1980, pp. 80-86.

Vollmer, Howard M. and Donald L. Mills, eds.
   1966 *Professionalization.* Englewood Cliffs, N.J.: Prentice-Hall.

Watson, Tony J.
   1976 "The Professionalization Process: A Critical Note." *The American So-
        ciological Review.* 24:599-608.

Weber, Max
   1946 *From Max Weber: Essays in Sociology.* Translated, edited, and with In-
        troduction by H. H. Gerth and C. Wright Mills. New York: Oxford
        University Press, esp. chs. 3, 7-9.

Wilensky, Harold L.
   1964 "The Professionalization of Everyone?" *The American Journal of So-
        ciology.* LXX, No. 2, pp. 137-158.

Yoder, John Howard
   1972 *The Politics of Jesus.* Grand Rapids: Eerdmans.

The Authors

David W. Augsburger, Goshen, Indiana, is associate professor of care at the Associated Mennonite Biblical Seminaries in Elkhart, Indiana. His most recent books deal with personal relationships, especially within Christian community.

Carl Bowman is presently doing doctoral studies in sociology at the University of Virginia.

Kenneth J. Brubaker, Rheems, Pennsylvania, is a family physician at the Norlanco Family Health Center.

Sheldon W. Burkhalter, Blooming Glen, Pennsylvania, is minister of the Word at the Blooming Glen Mennonite Church.

Al Dueck, Fresno, California, teaches psychology at Fresno Pacific College.

Myron Ebersole, Hershey, Pennsylvania, is director of the department of pastoral services at the Milton S. Hershey Medical Center. As a chaplain he has worked closely with terminally ill patients and their families.

Lawrence S. Eby, Millersburg, Ohio, is a family physician in a private practice.

S. Dale High, Lancaster, Pennsylvania, is president of High Industries, Inc.

Rodney E. Houser, Lancaster, Pennsylvania, teaches biology and physics at Lampeter-Strasburg High School.

Joanna Johnson, Lemoyne, Pennsylvania, directs family support services of Dauphin County.

Gordon D. Kaufman, Lexington, Massachusetts, is professor of theology at Harvard Divinity School.

Lois Yake Kenagy, Corvallis, Oregon, farms with her husband and is a church and community volunteer.

Gayle Gerber Koontz, Goshen, Indiana, is assistant professor of religion at Goshen College.

Ruth E. Krall, Goshen, Indiana, is director of student services and associate professor of nursing at Goshen College.

John A. Lapp, Goshen, Indiana, is provost and professor of history at Goshen College.

Ruth Detweiler Lesher, Pasadena, California, is a doctoral candidate and intern in psychology at Fuller Theological Seminary.

Ruth Hartzler Martin, State College, Pennsylvania, is director of nursing services at Centre Community Hospital.

Freeman J. Miller, Philadelphia, Pennsylvania, is pastor of the Diamond Street Mennonite Church and president of Diamond Street Community Center.

J. B. Miller, Jr., Sarasota, Florida, is executive vice-president of Gulf Coast National Bank.

Marlin E. Miller, Goshen, Indiana, is professor of theology and president of Goshen Biblical Seminary, Elkhart, Indiana.

José M. Ortiz, Goshen, Indiana, is associate general secretary of the Mennonite Church General Board, responsible for Latin concerns.

Nancy Fisher Outley, Landenberg, Pennsylvania, is social service director of the Women's Alternative Center in Media, Pennsylvania.

Howard Raid, Bluffton, Ohio, is a retired but continuing part-time professor of accounting and business at Bluffton College.

Calvin W. Redekop, Waterloo, Ontario, is professor of sociology at Conrad Grebel College and the author of numerous Mennonite sociological studies.

Carl N. Rutt, Sioux Falls, South Dakota, is associate professor of psychiatry at the University of South Dakota School of Medicine.

Theron Schlabach, Goshen, Indiana, is professor of history at Goshen College and editor of the "Mennonite Experience in America" history writing project.

Wallace and **Evelyn Shellenberger** live in Paoli, Indiana. Wallace is a physician; Evelyn is a family nurse practitioner.

Phil M. Shenk, Washington, D.C., is an editor of *Sojourners Magazine.*

Elaine Stoltzfus, Agnes, Kentucky, is a volunteer reading teacher.

LeRoy S. Troyer, South Bend, Indiana, is an architect with the LeRoy Troyer and Associates firm.

Frank G. Ward, Kansas City, Kansas, is pastor of the Rainbow Boulevard Mennonite Church.

A. Grace Wenger, Leola, Pennsylvania, is a retired English professor, a teacher of English as a second language, and writer.

The Editors

Donald B. Kraybill is the author of *Our Star-Spangled Faith* and the award-winning *Upside-Down Kingdom.* He is associate professor of sociology at Elizabethtown College in Pennsylvania, currently involved in research and writing on nuclear war. (*Facing Nuclear War,* Herald Press, 1982). The father of two daughters, he is a member of the Elizabethtown Church of the Brethren.

Phyllis Pellman Good, Lancaster, Pennsylvania, is the editor of *Festival Quarterly* and director with her husband, Merle, of The People's Place, an arts center near Lancaster. Trained as an English teacher, she is the author of *Paul and Alta* and coauthor of *20 Most Asked Questions About the Amish and the Mennonites.* She is a member of Landisville Mennonite Church and the mother of Kate and Rebecca.